THE WHATEVER LIFE HACK

Three Secret Biblical Investments
for Successful Living

By Mike G. Williams

THE WHATEVER LIFE HACK!

Three Secret Biblical Investments for Successful Living

by Mike Williams

ISBN:978-1951340018

Copyright © 2019 Cover design by Gerald Brown

For more information on this book and the author, visit:
www.MikeWilliams.tv

Various Scripture quotations are paraphrases or direct translations from earliest known texts and variably compared to other translations of Holy Scripture as determined by the author. Please refer to the version of your choice for comparison, scrutinization, and contextual accuracy.

Library of Congress Cataloging-in-Publication Data

Williams, Mike

THE WHATEVER LIFE HACK!

Three Secret Investments For Successful Living Mike Williams, 1st ed.

Printed in the United States of America

Mike G. Williams

Acknowledgments

Special thanks to my wife and family who allow me to write when the urge hits me. Hopefully, we will have a one-year writing hiatus. This time I mean it.

Thanks to every person who has demonstrated and proved the Law of Intentional Investment in my own life. You are the proof in the pudding.

Thanks to Renovate Publishing Group for their undying resolve to help the local churches be revitalized. You inspire us all.

Thanks to the people who are willing to let me pour into their life. I am merely a fellow traveler trying to share which roads suited me best. Maps are good.

Thanks to Rick Steves for hour of delightful touring through Europe via DVD. That boxed set was a great investment. If you ever want to trade occupations, I'm available for travel.

Thanks to Grammarly®, editors, and attentive volunteer proofreaders. Where were you when I started writing fifteen books ago?

Thanks to CupsMission.com, you allow me to practice what I preach.

CONTENTS

Foreword

Mike Williams has done it again. His newest book THE WHATEVER LIFE HACK: Three Secret Biblical Investments for Successful Living is another great read full of humor and blessed with practicality from scripture.

The author says in his introduction, "Can you keep a secret? I certainly hope so. This book contains one of the best-kept secrets of the entire Bible. Our postmodern culture would refer to this secret as a life-hack. For those of you who are from the generation where a hack; was second-rate comedian, you might want to get an online dictionary. Today, a LIFE-HACK is a shortcut to success." That is a challenging word and one full of insight, for the person who desires to become everything the Lord desires in one's life. The genius of this work is found in Chapter One as it asks the question what do you want to put in your bucket? The totally organic nature of this book leads one from chapter to chapter growing in the tools to make wise decisions for a better life.

Mike G. Williams is a comedian at heart. He finds humor in just about every situation. Spend a day with Mike, and you will spend a day with a very serious… crazy guy! Using that unique giftedness, Mike helps church congregations experience the joy of generosity. Mike has been called a comedian. Rightfully so as he garnered a Comedian of The Year award from the Gospel Music Association

Dove Awards in 2017, and written material for some pretty big names in the business. He is extraordinarily improvisational and will make you laugh, any time - anywhere. Beyond the humor, Mike is a serious soul who uses humor to keep the mind awake long enough to hear the message.

Mike is an "edu-tainment specialist," willing to use media, art, humor, music, drama, green chilis, and unauthorized graffiti, to teach the great truth of God's love. Every pastor ought to read this book and invite this man in to speak in your church. Mike is refreshing and awe inspiring. He has a humorous and encouraging spirit.

Dr. Tom Cheyney, Founder & Directional Leader
The Renovate Group; The Renovate National Church Revitalization Conferences

Invitation and Invocation

Invitation

I invite you to read something far from my normal humorous word crafting. Those of you who are familiar with my daily writings might find the style of this book a little less sarcastic and savory than others. It will be no less salient. I offer no apologies. Behind the humor has always been a deeper understanding for those who had ears to hear. This book is my personal observation of a real-life discoverable phenomenon. I need to contribute to the conversation.

It is a very jeopardous occupation, that of writing material that can alter a person's life. It is even more portentous, even daring, to speak for God, as the material contained here is declared to be mined from our Old and New Testaments of faith. I take on this challenge with humility and caution. I have done my best to avoid anything that could be considered hyperbole or auxesis. Nevertheless, staying true to my own conscience, you may find a few humorous notes in here as well. Enjoy.

Invocation

How fearful an occupation is the writing of biblical commentary, O Lord, as it shapes the way others look at You. May my words be faithful and true. May every genuine concept, stick to the heart and soul of the reader. May anything of myself fall away.

Make me faithful to my calling, O Great Architect of Truth, Poetry, and Drama. Let me be diligent to polish human stones for your praise. Allow your Spirit to stir the heart of every reader. May we all more suitably receive the reward, the crown of life. Through grace, may I be included as well.

May these words shoulder a transformative effect on those who read it, and those who come after them. May each life be blessed to be a greater blessing to others. As we bless others, may that act be an aroma of worship rising to your throne.

Amen, and amen.

Introduction

Bless the Lord, O my soul,
and don't forget any of His benefits.
-Psalm 103:2

Can you keep a secret? I certainly hope so. This book contains one of the best-kept secrets of the entire Bible. Our postmodern culture would refer to this secret as a life-hack. For those of you who are from the generation where a "hack" was second-rate comedian, you might want to get an online dictionary. Today, a *LIFE-HACK* is a shortcut to success. And success is what we all want!

life-hack
/ ˈlīf ˌhak/

noun INFORMAL

1.   A strategy adopted to manage one's time more efficiently.
2.   A less expensive natural product that works better than a store product.
3.   A more excellent fix that will cost you less money.

You are holding a surprisingly serious, biblically inspired, life-investment strategy book, delivered from the pen of a very fun-loving individual. If it were a movie it would most certainly declare itself to be based on actual events. Most importantly, from the truth of this book, my life-investments have turned out pretty good thus far. That success has been based on a lesser known *life-hack*, an often-overlooked law found in the Old and New Testaments. Let me tell you how this started.

I graduated from High School in 1980. Parachute pants and Members Only jackets® were all the rage. Great bands like The Knack, The Electric Light Orchestra, and Gloria Gaynor, were giving way to Madonna, Culture Club, Duran Duran, Bryan Adams, The Clash, and The Pet Shop Boys. Sting was still with The Police, and U2's Bono had not yet become the icon of charity around the world or given the Pope a pair of his sunglasses. At the time U2 was still trying to find what they were looking for. Boy George was considered weird back then, whereas now he would fit in perfectly. We listened to our music on an ultra-modern device called a Sony Discman®. It was a cumbersome portable CD player about the size of a personal pan pizza and weighed in at what felt like seventeen pounds. Carrying it was a small workout. It featured an anti-skip feature capable of draining the eight required double A batteries in about fifteen minutes. I paid over well one-hundred dollars for my first one and used four-hundred dollars in AA batteries the first year. The technology of those days I would rather forget.

In my junior year of high school, The Clash re-introduced my generation to a song written back in 1962 by Sonny Curtis. Sonny was not running from the police when he wrote the rock and roll classic "I Fought the Law and the Law Won." The young songwriter hadn't had any run-in with the authorities. He was merely letting truth inspire his creative juices on a dusty Texas afternoon. Sonny recorded the song with his band, The Crickets, shortly after the death of their frontman, Buddy Holly. Many artists have covered those amazingly accurate words knowing the law eventually wins, *unless you are a well-funded politician.*

I fought the law and the law won. ## *-Sonny Curtis*

Do a Google search on laws and in less than a second Google will return a million different suggestions. There are no shortages of local laws, state laws, federal laws, and international laws. There are crazy laws, strange laws, and stupid laws. There are natural laws and scientific laws. Our spinning globe has no shortage of laws.

My family recently enjoyed a trolley tour of Savanah, Georgia. General Oglethorpe founded it as a unique colony to separate the Spanish in Florida from the "others" in the more acceptable northern states above. He laid out a beautiful city grid with 22 squares, 20 of which still exist today. He instituted three basic laws for this new coastal colony. There would be no slaves, no hard alcohol, and no lawyers. *Depending on your profession, you might find those laws rather refreshing.* This South Georgia coast was often the American home of the noted Evangelist John Wesley. He is often remembered for his interesting statement, "I am going to Georgia to save the heathen, but who Oh Lord will save me?"

The three pigs are being sued by the Big Bad Wolf. Apparently, he twisted his ankle while trying to blow their house down. He hired a lawyer!

Any search engine will deliver a list of laws that make no sense but somehow made perfect sense when they were instituted. In Alabama, it's against the law to take a bath in a public fountain. I'm glad that one is in the books. In Goodyear, Arizona, there is a law against spitting in public. Apparently, in private, you can spit away, but in public, you could be arrested for clearing your pipes. As I type these words, I am preparing to board a plane for Chico, California. There they boast a law declaring that anyone possessing a nuclear bomb will be subject to a five-hundred-dollar fine. I will thus leave my nuclear devices at home, as I don't have a spare five-hundred dollars on me today. Colorado has a law against personal catapulting. Really? Was this ever a problem? Pretty much if you use a catapult to hurl yourself over the side of a mote, the landing itself should be punishment enough. In Connecticut, a pickle must bounce. These people take their sandwich toppings very seriously. A 1961 Georgia law prohibits eating fried chicken with utensils. Chick-Fil-A® and Zaxby's® could save a lot on their plastic utensil costs if Georgia's officers enforced this law. On the other side, Hawaii's legal system has banned all large roadside billboards as they distract from the natural beauty. Now

I might agree with this one unless I'm hungry and looking for the nearest Cracker Barrel restaurant. *This insight might lead Newark, New Jersey to promote larger billboards.*

Have you ever seen the information tags sewn into the side of every pillow and mattress sold in the United States? It gives the highly valuable information about the fire-retardant factors, the born-on date, and material composition of the item. *You never know when you are going to wake in the middle of the night and need to know those things.* Many comedians tell jokes about the inherent ramifications of actually removing these informational "DO NOT REMOVE UNDER PENALTY OF LAW" informational tags from a mattress or pillow. Has anyone ever been arrested for breaking that law? I can't imagine being grilled in prison as to my crime of murder, car theft, or bank robbery. "No… I removed a label from a mattress and the next thing you know the police were busting through my door on Live PD." You can understand how that particular offense could move you down in the jailhouse pecking order. *You better learn to make a shiv.*

On the other hand, we do have real, almost organic, natural laws. Sometimes they are referred to as scientific laws. Most likely, the first to come to your mind is the law of gravity. Jolly old Isaac Newton declared, "If you drop an apple from the top of a building, the law of gravity says it is going to go splat!" Isaac Newton didn't make the law; he observed it and wrote it down. Natural laws exist whether or not we know they exist.

Return to an era in which humankind, including the church leaders, believed the earth was flat. A theory making a great comeback with conspiracy buffs, and Facebook friends who have been recently baker acted. The universal law of gravitation keeps them all firmly grounded to our spinning ball though they did not or do not understand it. Every natural law is [always] in play. Gravity was once an unexplainable secret, an unknown, a mystery until Newton published his hypothesis. Since that day we have been refining its usage, and now we use gravitational force to catapult rockets into the outer reaches of earth's solar system. The same energy that keeps us grounded helps us reach the moon with less fuel. *Outside of Colorado, there is no universal catapult law.*

With simple ease, we can discover the law of motion. You might be able to quote it from your fourth-grade public school earth science class, or your second-grade homeschool science class. It says, "An object in motion tends to stay in motion, and objects standing still will tend to keep still. *I can prove this law by pointing out the life-long stagnancy of my brother in law.* Natural laws remain in effect under all circumstances.

There is the law of cause and effect. Every action creates a reaction. My son defined this saying, "Dad, this means if you eat a lot of fat greasy food, you become a fat greasy dude." *I reminded him I had a swift paddle and objects in motion tended to stay in motion.*

Laws are laws. They happen. Whether we appreciate them or not, they are in place. I need a *Laws Happen* bumper sticker. I might put *Laws Happen* on a billboard, but not in Hawaii. Natural laws radically improve our lives. Many of the laws (axioms/truths) are revealed to us from farther back than Sir Isaac Newton, or Thomas Hobbes, the teachers of Greek philosophy, *or the Professor on Gilligan's Island.* They are continually illuminated through a book found inside many hotel nightstands around the world. Indeed, this book is a free app on most everyone's cell phone. It is a book of the highest wisdom. This book exposes us to some immutable and unbreakable laws. This book reveals some ancient secrets and even an eternal life-hack. When you discover these amazing secrets in your Bible and act on them, your life will never be the same.

Before you discard a law, ask why it was put there in the first place.

Now when I say the "L" word (law) or the "R" word (rule) publicly, members of our culture tend to wince. There is an uneasy feeling that sweeps a room when you bring up anything to do with absolutes. We don't like laws, rules, or absolutes unless they are stacked in our favor. We are in a grace era. In today's religious society, God is described as a gentler God than he was in times past. *I guess thousands of years of working with people wears on you.* I know my parents have become more tolerant and amicable than they were thirty years ago.

The bicycle

A boy wanted a new bicycle. His mom told him to pray and ask Jesus to bring him a bicycle for Christmas only six months away. The next day the young man road a new bicycle to school. His best friend wanted to know what prayer he used to receive a new bicycle so quickly. He told his friend. "I didn't pray. I ripped-off the bicycle from Walmart. You could pray for six months and still never receive a bike. But I remember my pastor saying God would forgive whatever we've done in an instant if we just prayed. I took the pray-n-ride option."

I recently blogged, If the Ten Commandments were written today, they would be referred to as *The Three Suggestions*. Those suggestions would include, don't run with scissors if you are not coordinated, don't text and drive unless it is essential, and don't kill anybody unless they are an idiot and driving under the speed limit at rush hour. *The last suggestion delivered with a humorous New Jersey mafia voice.*

I am a grace guy. I believe in the unfathomable grace of God manifest toward all people. The children's song ranted it well, "Red and yellow, black or white, they are precious in His sight." God's grace given to humanity baffles the mind and causes me to fall prostrate before His overwhelming generosity and forgiveness. *Don't let the humor file me into a legalistic drawer. I am not.* I do believe that a good understanding of natural God-given laws gives anyone an advantage.

Anyone who listens to instruction will prosper.
Blessed is the one who trusts in the Lord.
-Proverbs 16:20

We are all lawbreakers by nature. This is why the criminalization of something, never wholly stops it. Back in the early 1900's they quickly discovered prohibition increased the number of speakeasy establishments there were. Good girls love bad boys, and bad boys like to make good girls go bad. Born in the heart of humankind is an evil streak (Jeremiah 17:9). Only when we receive a new nature that we can begin to [battle] our lawbreaking predisposition. Even then it is an uphill battle between our old outlaw self and our new self.

Welcome to our present society. We desire for [others] to have laws and fences, but we prefer to be the more [free-range] chickens of our culture. *Unfortunately, the future is not that great for free-range chickens.*

Give a little love, laughter, or kindness,
and you receive a lot of love, laughter,
and kindness in return.

Let me shift from foundational gears and get to our life-hack. Birthed into the core of everything I have observed in life is the rarely mentioned Law of Intentional Investments. *This law used wisely is a super life-hack!* Those who share love receive more love in return. Those who give grace, receive greater grace in return. Those who plant kindness harvest a wealth of kindness in return. Conversely, those who fling hatred receive more hatred in return. Those who give others grief receive greater grief in return. Those who advance discord receive a plethora of strife coming back at them. Don't let the simplicity distract you. I have found this concept to be much more significant than it seems. I promise you that the depth of this law will change your life.

Man cannot change a single law of nature, but he can put himself into such relations to natural laws that he can profit by them.
-Edwin Grant Conklin[1]

In the secular world, one might hear this life-hack referred to as karma. There are earthly words for everything. That doesn't make the spiritual basis without merit. Look at the great Prayer of Jesus (Matthew 6:9-13). A great example takes place in the prayer Jesus taught us to pray. There is clearly one reciprocal request.

Forgive us our debts, as we also have forgiven our debtors. (NIV)

Forgive us our sins, as we have forgiven those who sin against us. (NLT)

---

[1] https://todayinsci.com/C/Conklin_Edwin/ConklinEdwin-Quotations.htm

Forgive us our trespasses, as we also have forgiven those who trespass against us. (OEV)

Notice the wording of our Lord's instruction very carefully. Each noted version of the phrase asks God to grant us forgiveness, in [response] to what we [have already] done. We are to be the one who forgives first. As we plant human forgiveness, divine forgiveness will come to us. God's forgiveness is the greatest… the largest… the most potent dose of forgiveness available. Forgiveness can be discovered within the seed of eternal life. Stop! Could there be more to this reciprocal effort?

Whatever seed you plant, you will also harvest.
-Galatians 6:7

Whatever you sow you reap is an unchanging axiom of God as observed in Paul's letter to the Galatians, and many other places in scripture. This verse is often used as a warning to those who would sow seeds of evil, reminding them they would eventually reap more evil. But follow the underlying logic. You receive back to you, *whatever* you planted. It did not limit the outcome of planting and harvest to specific items. In every biblical translation cataloged it makes the sowed [item] universal. *Whatever!* Anything! Your choice. *Pick a card - any card!* Whatever means whatever! It is a biblical law of intentional investment. Did you hear the word biblical? Did you hear the word law? Did you hear the word whatever?

What if whatever could mean whatever for you?

I intend to prove to you the law (life-hack) of Intentional Investment is a biblical law written into the very fabric of all creation. Use it wisely, and you will experience one of the earliest observed secrets of God working in your favor.

My promise

I intend to prove to you that God's unchanging Law of Intentional Investment, guarantees that your joyful generous ventures into people, purposeful projects, and His church will be returned to you with generously increased proportions. Those blessings will be in this life and the one to come. Those returned blessing will prepare you to be a blessing again.

There are no secrets that enough time does not reveal. You also have cable news to contend with!

A great secret is like an undiscovered law. It is always trying to find the light of day. It is always working, all the time, whether we comprehend it or not. However, when we find out what the secret is, and how the secret works, we can use it to our advantage. And hopefully for the benefit of the entire world. The Law of Intentional Investment has been for many a well-kept secret. Some have been afraid of it for various and less than theological reasons.

The hunter hopes the prey have done their job and multiplied. Hopes his detection avoidance suit is superior and his aim is sure. Hopes the randomly discovered animal will be edible and legal.
Whereas, a farmer plants the seed of his own choosing, waters the seed, weeds the garden, and receives the greatly multiplied crop. Let someone else run around looking for furry objects.
Wisdom belongs to the farmer.
-Seth Godin, This is Marketing[2]

In the book Rich Dad - Poor Dad, Robert T. Kiyosaki[3] declares that rich dads teach their children how to repeatedly invest their money to make investments work [for] them. Whereas, Poor dads demonstrate to their children a system of consuming their own investment seed. Kiyosaki teaches you don't have to earn a high income to be rich when you systematically let your money work for you. We could all learn a lot from his book. His principles could have been ripped from pages of the Bible. I am grieved the modern church has not boldly broadcast these biblical principles earlier. Nevertheless, now they are back.

I believe you have the mental aptitude to join our journey into the generous reciprocating heart of God. This teaching is not narcissistic theology. As a

---

[2] C.f. www.sethgodin.com. I highly recommend everything written by Seth Godin. This quote is paraphrased from his latest best seller This Is Marketing. His book The Purple Cow was an entrepreneurial game changer.
[3] C.f. www.richdad.com

Christ-follower, it is not mine to self-serve. It is mine to seek what my Creator has planned for me. It is mine to walk humbly with my God. However, we can walk humbly and victoriously at the same time. This book will give you observable biblical axioms for [total-life] success strategy. You will discover that investments come in many colors other than green. Welcome to the beautiful and bountiful Law of Intentional Investments. You are going to enjoy it here.

Introduction Conversation & Action

1. What is your least favorite state or federal law?

2. What law would you change if you could?

3. Share your favorite cooking or cleaning hack?

4. What sentence, paragraph, or idea from this Introduction do you most want to talk about?

5. Of the scripture verses listed in this Introduction, which would be most beneficial to memorize?

6. Before reading the next chapter, make a list of the areas of need you genuinely have in your life and family. Keep that list close as we discover together.

Chapter One
Here's Your Bucket

The story has been told for many years about a man leading his old horse across a desert. He is sunburnt, dry, and parched. Both he and his horse are badly in need of water. Every step is a strain on both of them. They come to an old red farm-style water pump out in the middle of the sand. Was it a mirage? *I have no idea who put it there. Please remember this is an old story, and old stories were not required to give you the story in context.*

Next to this old red water pump was a bucket full of water. *I understand in reality; a bucket of water would have evaporated in a matter of days.* Next to this old red water pump and bucket was a crude wooden sign declaring, "You have two options, you can drink this bucket of water and go a little farther into the desert, or you can use this bucket of water to prime the water pump and receive all the water you need for the rest of your journey. Please leave a full bucket of water for the next thirsty person and horse in need." Can you feel the dilemma of the story? Can you feel the fear and the need for a trust factor or faith factor?

If our hypothetical man in the desert were you, would you have consumed the water or taken the life hack and invested in the pump? *I know what the horse would have done. Horses are beautiful, but they do not read signs.*

I realize this was a male narrative. I certainly do not intend to leave out the possibility this story could have also been about a woman walking in the desert. My wife

27

has since reminded me that a woman would not have been too proud to stop and ask directions back at the beginning of the desert and most likely would have never been in that spot. I reminded her how she most certainly could miss even a boisterous GPS telling her to turn while talking to a friend on the cell phone (happened last week), but would be better off than a man because her purse alone would carry enough sustenance to move her and the children through the desert.

In our bucket and pump story, there were a few absolutes in place. You had to trust the one who left the water bucket before you was not lying to you. You had to trust the water pump would work after all the time in the desert sun. You had to trust that clean water was down in the well. You had to understand the Law of Hydraulics. Only by pouring your bucket of water in the top of the pump, would allow the old leather reed to moisten, and create a seal inside the pipe. Then you could pull the water from deep below the ground. Without an investment of the water, there was no possibility the old pump would work. There were laws and trust factors involved in this story. There was action (labor) needed. The thirsty man had a choice, and he needed to choose quickly and correctly. The man had a dilemma.

Their life proves the work of the law
is written on their hearts
-Romans 2:15a

Everybody person needs to make life choices. Do we desire the limits of our current bucket of whatever, or do we want many buckets? We all come into this world with a bucket of resources, gifts, and talents. What we do with our bucket of resources determines whether we receive additional buckets.

Oh, how I love Your law! I meditate on it all day long. Your commands are always with me and make me wise. I have more insight than all my teachers, and I have more understanding than the elders, for I choose to obey Your precepts.
-Psalm 119:97-99

I had a pastor friend who was perhaps the most influential mentor in my spiritual growth. He was a rather animated guy and often used engaging illustrations as his method of training young believers. He was the first to introduce me to the story of the thirsty man. One day my mentor friend blurted, "Do you like corn?" I responded with, "I love corn. Yellow corn, white corn, corn on the cob, corn off the cob, cream corn, shoepeg corn, corn chips, corn tortillas, corn flakes, Crispy Corn Chex, corndogs, cornbread, and chicken corn chowder. Asking a fat guy if he likes corn is liking asking fish if they like water." He laughed at my rant and pulled from his top left desk drawer an old mason jar filled with dried kernels of seed corn. Twisting the top, he shook one kernel into his hand and retightened the lid. He said, "I now give you a lifetime supply of corn." He took a single kernel of corn and placed it in my hand, and I laughed, "That isn't enough corn for one meal. It isn't even corn. This is just a kernel of corn." He responded, "No, that is Corn. One kernel of corn is enough corn to feed you all the corn you will ever need for the rest of your life. All you have to do is plant this seed in some fertile ground, let it rain, then work crazy-hard to collect bushels of corn. If you plant one little corn, you will harvest at least 1200 or more little corns. Plant 1200 little corns, and harvest 1 million 440,000 or more little corns. Plant 1,440,000 corns and harvest 1 Billion 278 million or more corns! Plant your corn and let God do what God does with corn." He was teaching me a life hack that has served me very well ever since.

He continued, "Mike, I have taught you about the love of God, the Grace of God, and the mercy of God. I have taught you how your response to God's grace gives you an all-access pass to eternity with Him. I have taught you many of His laws, His reoccurring axioms, the secret truths in both the old and the new testament, and how the utilizing those truths bring great blessing to your life. I have taught you how to invite others to faith in Jesus, and you have experienced the joy of sharing your faith. I have taught you how honoring your parents brings a blessed life to you as a gift from God. I have taught you how to delight yourself in the Lord, and in return, He will bring you the desires of your heart. Today I will teach you a physical, tangible, and immutable axiom! If you use the law, it will change your future. It is a law as real and sure as the law of gravity. In fact, like gravity, it works for Christians as well as anyone who will use it! It is the secret Law of Farming. This law can become for you the most profitable, helpful, and biblical law this side of heaven." I was intrigued. I had not heard of the Law of Farming in Sunday School. I have since come to know it, teach it, and write about it, as the Law of Intentional Investment. In this culture, I know it as the whatever life-hack.

The Law of Intentional Investment

Together we will observe this Law of Intentional Investment throughout the Bible and prove to ourselves that it works in [every] aspect of our life today. Let's define the process/operation of this law using prevalent, secular word points.

1. Identify a genuine physical, emotional, spiritual, or financial need in your own life.

2. Joyfully and intentionally invest a portion of whatever you need.

3. Experience your needs met in an increased harvest.

Most of us understand there is a difference between random giving and intentional investing. If I threw money from a moving kayak, nobody in their right mind would call it investing. Hopefully we all understand the basics of investing.

I am not a financial genius... but I have a guy! Jimmy works with a highly trusted Christian financial investment organization called Thrivent Financial.[4] Their scope of membership is limited to proclaimed Christ-following individuals. They invest much of what other companies keep in fees back into the Christian community. Like many of you, I place a small [intentional] portion of my income into a retirement account. The investment firm waters and nourishes my investment. In due time I will receive an increase on what I planted in the first place. They work with retirement funding, whereas God is a [whatever] investment banker. God can multiply anything and everything. Let me give you some crazy examples.

WHATEVER YOU PLANT!

Have you ever thought of worship as being an investment? Let's define the word worship. It is commonly defined as attributing value and worth to someone. In our case, we would be assigning worth and value to our great and glorious God. Would you agree we declare value and worth to God as we worship? Do you believe our worship is a sweet aroma to God? Do you believe God enjoys or appreciates it?

We reunite each Sunday to receive doctrine, instruction, reproof, and even correction from the scripture. We connect weekly to be encouraged by other shareholders in faith. We bring our frail, often off-key

---

[4] www.thrivent.com. Investing in any company comes with risks to you as the investor. Though the author is extremely satisfied with the investment services provided to his non-profit organization, the author is making no promises to the service you can experience through this organization.

voices, and cry out to God in worship. Now the phraseology I am about to use is going to be a little scary. Here goes… as we attribute worship to God, He worships us! He reminds us we are valued, we are His children, and we have been given [worth and worthiness] through the gift of grace.

**As we declare honest worth to God,
he brings genuine worth to us.**

This is worship returned! Pain relief often comes in response to worship. Peace comes in response to worship. Inspiration comes in response to worship. Answers come in response to worship. Healing often takes place in response to worship.

What happens when we intentionally honor, esteem, lift, and extol God? God responsively impacts and blesses our life in return. It changes our attitude too. As we worship, God stuff happens. As we [bless] Him, God [blesses] us back! Worship itself demonstrates intentional investment.

**We are the beautiful aroma of Christ to God
among others who are being saved.
-2 Corinthians 2:15a**

Christian music has enjoyed many wonderful minstrels. Many, I am thrilled to call my friends. In the '70s there rose a touring group named *Truth*. They traveled millions of miles and ate a lot of fast-food to sing the good news of Jesus. I remember one of their most beloved of songs. The words were rather repetitious, but so is the one song currently being sung around the throne of God if Revelation chapter seven is to be translated literally. *Apparently, God is okay with repetition as long as it is with merit.* This vocal band's words rang out in six-part harmony, "We get lifted up, we get lifted up, we get lifted up - when we praise Him..." Worship is reciprocal. I have yet to meet a passionate, intentional worshipper who did not receive more from worship than they put into it. *And we worship without time limit unless we need to vacate the building for the second service.*

Whoever adheres to God's perfect law receives freedom, and continuing in that law, without forgetfulness, will have blessings in whatever they do. -James 1:25

I wholeheartedly believe the act of swinging a hammer as we build a house for a third-world family is worship. Swinging a hammer to help a first world neighbor can also be an act of worship if it is done with a worshipful intention. The action of worship is not limited to Hillsong® or Bethel® music, raised hands, a good band, motion lighting, a great subwoofer system, and skinny jeans. Giving worth to God can include our intentional care of His creation, which could include nature, the environment, the animals, and our bodies. Let's worship the Creator forever! In response, we will feel His presence and experience His touch. The whatever we invest can be worship!

WHATEVER YOU PLANT!

Talk about going from heavy to light... here we go. Ladies, you are going to enjoy this illustration. My wife knows a rather well-dressed lady. This lady has a unique approach to her clothing acquisitions. This lady intentionally goes through her closet and finds clothing she believes would be perfect for another lady, a lady who is often much less fortunate than her. She gives (plants) the older outfits secretly in the act of planting into another woman. Then she plans a shopping trip, specifically praying for the Lord lead her to the right place, to find the right dress, in the right size, for the right price. She claims it works. Who am I to doubt her? My wife says she has the most excellent outfits of any woman in our church, and she does it on a minuscule budget.

So it is possible that clothing, shoes, and accessories are included in the [whatever] you plant results. I am merely giving you a testimony from another. But if a law is universal, and whatever means whatever. Why wouldn't it include clothing? *The men might want to invest by planting a firearm.*

WHATEVER YOU PLANT!

Have you ever faced an angry, loud, and getting louder person? If you reciprocate anger and volume in return, they become more enraged and louder. If you plant quietness, you de-escalate the situation and receive a quieter response. When I speak to audiences, often I am the first guy on the podium, and the audience is still having table conversations. I have found the best way is to start whispering and let the room come to me. I plant whispers. Whatever means whatever!

WHATEVER YOU PLANT!

Although mentioned earlier, consider forgiveness in our [whatever] investment narrative again. It seems that all of God's systems flow from a plant and harvest investment program.

> *Forgive others first, and after you have forgiven others, you will receive forgiveness from the Father for your sins. -Mark 11:25*

Through the corroborating evidence given to us in the prayer example of Jesus, and many verses throughout the New Testament, we can conclude that the Law of Intentional Investment (harvest) includes the [whatever] of forgiveness. *At this point, highly intelligent people might begin to see a pattern developing.*

WHATEVER YOU PLANT!

I recently watched a video documentary about a single mom who was upside down financially. Her pastor had been, in her words "harping" about tithing to the church. The church leadership offered a 90-day investment guaranty. She was instructed to tithe systematically for 90 days, and if she did not experience her financial situation improving, the church would refund all she invested. She tried it and saw a supernatural change in her economic condition. Now she continues to intentionally invest because she knows it works.[5]

WHATEVER YOU PLANT!

Here is where it became hard for me. My mentor friend talked to me about intentionally investing a portion of my talent resources, my knowledge resources, and my financial resources. Then I would supposedly observe for myself what God would do with it. I was okay with sharing my talent and sharing my knowledge (what little I had back then), but I was hung up on the financial portion.

I was experiencing my first real, full-time, everyday drudgery of a low paying job. Advancement at this business was limited. The owner would have to die and leave the place to me rather than his children. I couldn't see it happening. I remember my take-home pay was one-hundred and eleven dollars for every week of sweating in the hot sun. One-hundred and eleven dollars seemed to be a lot at the end of the first week, but then reality set in, and my long division reminded me my paycheck broke down to less than sixteen dollars a day. Could that buy food, insurance, and gas for my car? Could it pay for a great date night?

My friend wanted to teach me how to turn my talent, my knowledge, and my income into something

---

[5] richpraytor.com/index.php/videos/ Please note that I cannot promise your local church is offering the money-back guaranty program. Check your local listing for times and special offers.

greater. I thought I was getting ready to hear about a multi-level marketing opportunity. No, he was reinforcing the Law of Intentional Investment. This law would eventually change my life to this day.

I will write my laws upon their hearts and minds.
-Hebrews 10:16b

Admittedly, most of us don't like laws, rules, or absolutes, unless they are stacked in our favor. Good news, the Law of Intentional Investment is stacked in our favor. It is set up for nothing but a win-win for all participants. Forget this law, and you remain in the same place you are now. Utilize this law, and you move forward. The Law of Intentional Investment is the can of hair spray, a wooden match, and one electrical cord for MacGyver. God's law is our leg up.

When Calls the Wonder Bread

Let me tell you a sad story with a happy ending that was not inspired by a Hallmark movie. Wendy was an old widow woman. Her life had not panned out the way she hoped. Life had been hard. Her husband Bob had died ten years ago, and she was raising her son Ben alone. There was a drought in the land, and their little farm was not producing enough for them to sustain themselves. She had been selling off everything the family-owned to pay the bills, but an eviction notice was fresh on the front door, and the local sheriff had already given her the names of a local homeless shelter. Ending it all had crossed her mind several times, and if it weren't for her son Ben, it would undoubtedly have happened.

The day came, and Wendy knew she was going to have to send her son to a children's home and move to a shelter. She had just enough food to prepare them one final meal. There she would break the news to her son. Her ultimate plan was all laid out in her mind until the knock came at the door. Embarrassed to open the door as there was no furniture left inside, she cracked it only slightly. A familiar face came into view. It was her old pastor.

Before she could say a word, he groaned, "I am so thirsty, please give me a glass of water." She turned to retrieve some water from the kitchen when he spoke again, "And make me a little sandwich too, I am famished. I have been so swamped praying for the congregation all week." She began to cry, "Pastor, here is the whole truth. I have only enough food to prepare something for my son before I send him away and I... I... I die." The pastor implored, "This is an opportunity for you to plant what you need in the soil of another. Prepare me a sandwich. When you invest in my need, God will keep your refrigerator full."

Ouch! That seems rather selfish. This is a horrible story. Where is the happy ending? Do you think our widow woman made him a sandwich or told the pastor where he could store that sandwich? I know what I might have said. What would you have done? The parable you just read is not far removed from a real story involving the Prophet named Elijah.

The Lord communicated to Elijah, "Arise, go to Zarephath, and dwell there. I have ordained a widow there to feed you." When he came to the gate of the Zarephath, behold, a widow was there gathering sticks. He called to her and said, "Bring me a little water in a vessel, that I may drink." She accepted the task. Then he continued, "Bring me a little bread also." The widow replied, "As the Lord your God lives, I have nothing prepared, I only a handful of flour in a jar and a little oil in a jug. I am gathering these sticks that I may go in and prepare it for myself and my son, that we may eat it and die." Elijah responded, "Do not fear; go and make that meal, but first, make me a little cake and bring it to me, and then afterward make something for yourself and your son. For thus says the Lord, the God of Israel, 'The jar of flour shall not be spent, and the jug of oil shall not be empty, until the day this drought is over.'" And she went and did as Elijah said. And everyone in her household ate, as the jar of flour was not spent, neither did the jug of oil become empty.
-1 Kings 17:8-16

Wow! This poor widow plants a seed of flour and oil, based on her own need for flour and oil, into the soil of God's Prophet. Observe her resulting long term flour and oil, and life for her family. This was not a cash gift! There was not an offering plate involved. This was not a tithe! This was a muffin mix miracle. This was Intentional Investment…delivered!

We are observing how God takes our intentional investments, whatever those investments are (time, talents, gifts, skills, calling, love, emotions, and even money), and multiplies them. I will have to keep reminding you this book is not specifically about money, although many of the references from scripture contain illustrations using money. This factor proves the [whatever] works for finances too.

This book may be offensive to readers who are afraid to talk about personal blessings. If you think Jesus was giving hyperbole when he spoke about abundant life, this book will offend you. It is ironic how the universal Law of Intentional Investments will work for an atheist or an agnostic. In other words, atheists and agnostics are being blessed by this law, while some of God's beautiful people are afraid of it.

God's laws are universal. Use them for you, or they will be working against you.

We have all received a bucket of time, a bucket of talent, a bucket of resources, a bucket of education, a bucket of love, and the list could continue. Admittedly, some people received a bigger bucket of certain items than others. Nevertheless, we are all provided buckets and access to a pump. We even received a bucket of wealth. They say our U.S. population enjoys the rank of the wealthiest in the world. A recent Washington Post article[6] reminds us that the poorest among us are in still

---

[6] C.f.
https://www.washingtonpost.com/news/wonk/wp/2016/01/21

among the top 1% of the wealthiest people on the globe.

Our joy quotient in life is not limited to the amount or value of the buckets we start with. If the bucket and pump parable were real, and you were our person in the desert, would you have consumed the water in the bucket or trusted the pump? Seriously, what would you have done? Invest, or hoard? Will we hoard our few buckets or use them to harvest more buckets?

Chapter One Conversation & Action

1. What sentence, paragraph, or idea from this chapter do you most want to talk about?

2. Is the author taking the "whatever" to an extreme?
3. What was your first emotion to reading the modern-day widow story?

4. Of the scripture verses listed in this chapter, which would be most beneficial for us to memorize?

5. Before reading the next chapter, make a list of the top 3 "whatever" needs, you would hope this Intentional Investment hypothesis (at this point) could truly impact.

/you-might-be-among-the-richest-people-in-the-world-and-not-realize-it/?noredirect=on&utm_term=.0c0a6eef77bd.

Chapter Two
GOT SEEDS?

Rubik's Cube is a 3-D combination puzzle invented in 1974 by the Hungarian professor of architecture, Ernő Rubik. In 2014, I sat next to one of the Rubik's Cube World Champions on a flight from Atlanta to Seattle. He could solve any cube dilemma and return it to original in less than four seconds... blindfolded. *For three solid hours, he held a cube in his hand, closed his eyes, and solved the puzzle.* I inquired as to how he did it. He explained that I had to know the hack. In knowing the predetermined limitations of the cube's motion, one would merely maneuver from that advantage point for success. *Of course... laws and systems and hacks.* I didn't understand him either. I think he needs to get a real job.

When we understand the anchor points (laws and systems) of God's complete design, we can begin to use those points [unselfishly] for the greater good. I intend to prove to every reader how God takes [all] of our intentional investments, whatever those investments are, time, talent, knowledge, gifting, skill, calling, love, and yes even money... and multiplies it back to the joyful, intentional investor! And you will be able to do it blindfolded. *Let's get our cube on.*

If you are labeling me as some type of televangelist... I AM NOT! I will not conclude this book with a request for you to buy me a new jet, or limo, or condo. I am not going to ask you to help me feed hungry snowbirds living in aluminum houses in Florida. I certainly wouldn't mind the donation of a small well-maintained fishing boat if you have a spare one in the garage, with a substantial four-cycle outboard motor of course.

In the unlikely event that you have never heard the term before, a person suffering from Chrematophobia has a deep aversion, dread, or fear of money. This phobia affects their daily life. Many are psychologically afraid of the corrupting power of money. Others might fear financial failures and the responsibility money can bring. Some cases are related to a fear of germs from money handled by others. In general, Chrematophobia is a [rare] phobia affecting a handful of people around the world. *And most of them attend church.*

Some people believe mixing money and religion is wrong. At some point in their life, they knew a religious leader who turned out to be a thief, or a bad guy, or a closet Mike Huckabee or a Hillary Clinton supporter. Maybe they attended a church that talked about money every sermon. Perhaps they watched and supported some televangelist who used the money for an ungodly purpose. It happens. Nevertheless, you don't give up on driving because somebody sold you a bad car forty years ago.

The ungodly plumber

I once hired a "Christian plumber" to fix my broken toilet. Years later he left his family and became a drug addict. Does that make all plumbers evil? Does this mean I am giving up on indoor plumbing? *I remain pro indoor toilet.* The good news for both the Chrematophobics and the plumber distrusting, is this life hack is not exclusively about money. Eliminate money from your mind. *Wash your hands of it.*

Look at Paul's life hack observations as revealed in his second letter to the Christians living around the city Corinth. Let's explore first how God can multiply our non-monetary intentional investments. Read it well, as we are going to be breaking it down together in depth.

Remember this... a farmer who plants only a few seeds will harvest a small crop. But the one who sows generously will receive a bountiful crop. You must each decide in your heart how much to plant. And don't plant reluctantly or in response to pressure. For God loves a person who gives cheerfully. And God will generously respond with all you need. Then you will always have everything you need, and plenty left over to share with others. As the Psalmist penned, "They share freely and give generously to the poor. Their good deeds will be remembered forever." For God is the one who provides seed for the farmer that later becomes his bread. In the same way, God will provide for you and increase your resources, and produce a great harvest of repeated generosity in you. Yes, you will be enriched in every way so that you can always be generous. And when we take your gifts to those who need them, they will thank God. Two good things will result from this ministry of giving—the needs of the believers will

be met, and they will joyfully express their thanks to God. As a result of your sharing, they will give glory to God for your generosity to them. This will prove that you are obedient to the Good News of Christ. And they will pray for you with deep affection because of the overflowing grace God has given to you. Thank God for this gift!
-2 Corinthians 9:6-15

If I were writing that passage in the 21rst century I would conclude it with, thank God for revealing this amazing life hack. Let's chop these verses apart, one phrase at a time, and discern if there is any truth to this so-called law. Can we [observe] this law in operation in the world around us? I want to move this law from hypothesis to fact.

First Intentional Investment Observation
In God's Law of Intentional Investment, you impact the rate of return by the amount of seed you plant.

Let us continue to remember this foundational law can be implied to [whatever] you are planting, be it love, knowledge, friendship, whatever. If God's laws are universal and immutable, they work for money just as well as they work for love.

Remember this… a farmer who plants only a few seeds will harvest a small crop. But the one who sows generously will receive a generous crop. You must each decide in your heart how much to plant. -2 COR 9 v6-7b

You bring a spoonful of seed, and God returns a shovel of veggies. You bring a shovel of seed, and God returns a wheelbarrow of vegetables. You bring a wheelbarrow of seed, and God returns a truckload of veggies. This is what our financial friends refer to as ROI (return on investment).

The day my friend placed a single kernel of corn in my hand. He explained a single kernel of corn would produce 1200 or more duplicate corn(s) on one corn stalk. If God can do multiplication with corn, what can he do with other things? God multiplies the amount we invest - whatever we invest. God is the original investment banker. You find it everywhere in scripture! Do you need 120 beans? Then plant one bean! Do you need 64 ounces of tomatoes? Then plant one tiny, 120th of an ounce of tomato seed! Your pocket can hold enough tomato seeds to supply your favorite Italian restaurant for a century!

I'm sure Isaac Newton did many tests to verify his hypothesis for his natural laws beyond the apple drop test. I'm sure he experimented with everything from fruits to nuts, including dropping an Acme anvil from the top of a cliff that would later be used repetitiously in Roadrunner cartoons. Each time the universal law of gravity worked, and the apple, the orange, the chair, the paper, the water, the cat, and the anvil raced to the ground. The Law of Gravity is real!

Similarly, there is a discovery and testing process in spiritual-based laws. Look at how this intentional investment law may have been initially observed in the Garden of Eden. Adam and Eve started a small family and look at what happened. The human seed was planted and replanted. Though they did not have a pen to write it down as Newton did. Adam and Eve observed the garden system repeating. There is no better place to learn about the laws of planting one seed and getting back a thousand seeds than working than in a garden.

If two people from 4000 BC get a divorce, are they still cousins?

Sin eventually robbed the goodness of creation. God brought a flood to all but entirely abort mankind. But there was a boat! Noah took over and he and his three farm boys planted their seeds, and there are 7 billion of us today. Mankind knows how to plant.

Early herdsmen observed a few males of the herd coming together with a few females of the herd. Seed was exchanged, and the herdsmen received a greater heard. *Then they could trade a few of those sheep, goats, or alpacas for a nice wife in the village.*

One of the first financial [monetary] observations of God's Law of Intentional Investment was an act of thanksgiving from Abraham to God! Abraham chose to transfer a generous portion of his [entire] net worth to God through a priest named Melchizedek. Abraham (aka. Abram) blessed the priest Melchizedek, with 10% of his entire net worth. OUCH! I might have started at 2% and worked my way up after I observed increase.

But not Abraham. He gave 10% of everything. The Law of Intentional Investment continued blessing Father Abraham for his entire life. In fact, some might say [God's blessing] from that first financial investment has been increasing for the Abrahamic family ever since.[7]

Who was Melchizedek? Theologians don't know for sure. There is much speculation. Many believe he may have been a pre-incarnation of Jesus Christ (whatever that entirely means). Some say he was an angel representative from God brought to teach Abraham. There is no record of from where he came or to where he departed. He just was. And Abraham chose Melchizedek to be the initial point of religious investment. As Abraham gave offering (invested) into the soil of God through Melchizedek, he had a blessing poured out upon him, from God.

Offensive Truth

I was helping a Christian radio station recently with their Share-A-Thon. That is a yearly fundraising event all non-profit stations have to do to pay the electric bills. Christian radio may be free, but the operating costs are genuine. I suggested using some of the material from this very book. Encourage people to plant a seed of encouragement into their radio station and then receive great encouragement from the station in the years to come.

---

[7] C.f. Genesis chapter 14

The show host, whom I dearly love and respect, replied with a gentle hesitancy, "Ah, I don't know. We don't want to come off as a [name it - claim it] televangelist type of a place." [8] I completely understood his fears. However, it is a great shame when we have to bury the truth for fear of misunderstanding. What I am articulating is far - far – far from that doctrine. With any truth, there are those who misuse it. Think about it. Do self-serving people make the truth less truthful? *Does gravity make a bra company less altruistic?*

A few days later, I sat in my windowed office looking down on the city. I could see all of the skyscrapers below me, and the sun was rising beautifully behind it all. You see my office is often the window seat of a Delta airplane. With four million air miles under my belt, I usually receive an upgrade to an upfront seat. I was typing away on this very book when the Armani suit next to me took an interest. I explained the book for him in a straightforward five-sentence narrative. His response was interesting... and engaging, "Yes, the Principle of Reciprocity. When we invest generously in the common good, the cosmos gives back even more. Every business leader from Zig Ziglar to Henry Ford to Steve Jobs understands that axiom." Though my

---

[8]   C.f. The phrase "Name it and Claim it" was often attributed to itinerate preachers who were trying to garner money from their constituency by encouraging them to tell God what item they wanted, claim that item in faith, and then go out and buy it in faith. They were told God was duty bound to provide whatever they desired based on a promise of transcendent Abrahamic blessings. They were often told that their [claimed item] could be super-boosted by a large corresponding gift to the televangelist's own organization. This claim-ology is still prevalent today, although it has been rebranded many times for modern culture.

airplane acquaintance did not know it was a [biblical] law, he understood and respected the principle. There were most likely people in his business world who abused or maligned the principle, but it has not dissuaded the business world from participating. I would hope the Christian community could have the same intelligence. *Notice I used the word hope.*

**Whenever you feel 'short' or in 'need' of
something, give what you want first, and it will
come back in buckets. That is true for money, a
smile, love, friendship. I know it is often
the last thing a person may want to do,
but it has always worked for me.
-Robert T. Kiyosaki, Rich Dad, Poor Dad[9]**

People might say, "Brother, I don't desire a lot of money, I might become greedy. The Bible says money is the root of all evil." Stop half-quoting the Bible! The Bible does not declare money to be the root of all evil. Paul warned his young prodigy (1 Timothy 6:10) about the "LOVE OF MONEY" becoming the root of all evil. Money is just linen-paper, golden coins, or silver certificates. Money is an inanimate object! It can sway people to act irrationally or improperly, or it can build a children's hospital. Unfortunately, I have used it for both in times past.

One could say, "The root of all fatness is potato chips." Not true! Eating an entire family-sized chip bag every night causes fatness. Especially if there is onion

---

[9] https://www.richdad.com

dip involved. An entire truckload of Chips never hurt anyone until people decided to consume the whole load. Please note that baked lightly salted potato chips consumed at a moderate level are an excellent side to any sandwich. Amen!

Investing is good. Increase is good. Use the overflowing return to change the world. Use the overflow to demonstrate your thankfulness to God. Give it away if you desire. Feed the poor. Dress the naked. Heal the sick. *Buy a Corvette convertible… and take old ladies from the nursing home out for the afternoon.* It could be a ministry.

Some of you are new to intentional investment, or even the basics of trusting God. Consider there are people all around you, older members in your congregation of faith who have been financially investing in the kingdom for 40 years. People don't usually give for 40 years because something doesn't work - they give because something does. They invest because they have observed a return, over and over again. What is your need? Invest accordingly.

<u>First Intentional Investment Observation</u>
In God's Law of Intentional Investment, you impact the rate of return by the amount of seed you plant.

Chapter Three Conversation & Action

1. Are you any good at Rubik's cube?

2. Share any personal gardening type of story.

3. Share how you have observed the Principle of Reciprocity at work in the secular world.

4. Is the Principle of Reciprocity only operational for irreligious or unreligious people?

5. Have your past religious or denominational experiences taught you to be skeptical of this type of teaching?

6. What sentence, paragraph, or idea from this chapter do you most want to talk about?

7. Of the scripture verses listed in this chapter, which single scripture would be most beneficial to memorize?

8. In your spare time, consider how missing God's laws in the past has impacted your life. Consider what you would have done differently if you knew now what you didn't know then.

Chapter Three
Multiply by Joy

I have a friend who started a little service business many years ago. In doing so, like Abraham, he and his wife decided to put God to the test. Testing God is okay to do. In the book of Malachi, we are invited to participate in our own bucket-pump challenge.

Test this giving and receiving platform.
Prove that I will pour out an overflowing blessing
upon you. -Malachi 3:10

My friend and his wife decided to put God to the test, and joyfully gave 10% of their earnings to God through their local church, and God blessed their business. Soon after, he and his wife realized if God could increase their 10%, they could trust him with 11%. They started joyfully increasing their financial partnership investments by 1% every year. They can give more each year with [joy] because they experience the results of the investing more each year.

Don't share reluctantly or in response to pressure.
God loves those who share cheerfully.
-2 COR 9 v7b

Second Intentional Investment Observation
The attitude of our investment is a catalyst
for our return, so invest with joy.

Dr. D. James Kennedy, an influential pastor who was known around the world for his expository preaching, explained the original meaning for this [cheerful giving] concept. He believed it should have been translated as saying, "God loves a hilarious giver!" He believed our contemporary translations should articulate God's extreme love for every person who invests "hilariously" in a good cause.[10]

I know many financial investors and have been one myself for many years. There is something about a laughing investor. They invest more because they enjoy it. When you are sad about an issue, you tend to [donate] a small amount because you want your sad feeling to reside. You could receive the same relief by leaving the room and finding a distraction on the internet. When you are happy about being part of a significant and influential change you [invest] with joy and laughter in your heart. For me, giving/investing into a good cause brings a burst of almost sinister laughter, knowing my gift is going to whack the enemy in the face and take back what rightfully belongs to God. *There is your Whack-A-Mole fun!*

Give generously and do so without a grudging heart; then because of this, the Lord your God will bless you in all your work and in everything you put your hand to. -Deuteronomy 15:10

In 2011 my family helped establish a mission that feeds people living at a garbage dump and rescues young

---

[10] www.djameskennedy.org/

girls caught in the trap of human trafficking.[11] We have come to know some fantastic people on our journey in the Dominican and Haitian cultures. One is a young man who really knows how to demonstrate gratitude. You share a kindness with him, and you are going to know how grateful he is. He will find multiple ways to thank you. You will feel arms around you a week later and hear, "Brother, I just can't tell you enough of how much those shoes meant to me." There is never any question as to his thankfulness. In response, I subconsciously look for ways to bless him. His gratitude drives my heart to bless him more.

God works in you multiple ways to fulfill his most divine purpose. -Philippians 2:13

If I am created in the image of God, there is a good possibility our thankful reciprocation is a God trait too. We all love our children equally, at the core of our heart. However, there is always one child we find easier to bless. There is always one child who is more gratifying to give gifts because their face will gleam with excitement at the simplest of gifts. I have observed this same [desire to give back] in the very heart of God.

I Object!

Do I hear an objection? I should have long before now. Some would reveal you have tried this "sowing and reaping" life-hack stuff and it did not work. Well,

---

[11] CupsMission.com Cups mission serves the poorest of the poor Haitian and Dominican people.

maybe you hacked it wrong. Did you intentionally plant the exact crop you wanted to receive? Did you consider the time it takes for a crop to yield the bounty, or did you walk away in discouragement before the time of harvest? What was your planting attitude? Did you plow the field and weed it? Did you rent a tractor in expectation of a harvest? Were you equipped to receive the harvest? Was your farm upside down in a ditch of unprepared ignorance?

Would you arrive expectantly at a financial retirement planner's office on the day before you retired if you had not invested in the years before? This is how some have treated this wonderful reciprocating law. Some have impatiently left their harvest in the field and moved on. If you are throwing away the harvest, you can't blame the soil. *You don't show up at the Rubik's Cube match, having not practiced it for years.*

You say giving, He says Shareholding, I say investing. Can't we all get along?

This might be a great time to mention that the Law of Intentional Investment is not a replacement for a poor work ethic, ignorant investing, or frivolous spending. Some people can spend (or waste) faster than they can harvest. Stop it! Learn how to spend your newly harvested [whatever] wisely, and it will fill the barn. Some people are so far behind they will need a year or two of a good harvest to return back to zero. This is a job for Dave Ramsey, not me.[12]

Those who [wait] for the Lord [shall] renew their strength; they [shall] soar with wings as eagles; they [shall] run and not breath heavy; they [shall] walk and not faint. -Isaiah 40:31

The "wait" word is used once in the preceding verse. The "shall" word used four times in the verse. I am not an English major, but I believe those words express a [future] concept. They indicate a promised future outcome. Don't expect an interest check overnight any more than you would an overnight crop. Seeds have to germinate. It has to rain, nutrients from all of nature have to be absorbed into those vines and branches. Then you have to sharpen the hoe, fuel the combine, and clean the truck. It takes labor to retrieve the crops from the field. *As a side benefit, that wait time builds character.*

Prosperity will have a season...
but all the roots run deeper when it's dry.
-David Wilcox[13]

There is always a time factor, a germination factor, a stewing process. We must keep an [attitude] of joy as we wait on the return. Sometimes God is working in our

---

[12] DaveRamsey.com Dave Ramsey is often considered America's trusted voice on money. He is both a National best-selling author and radio host teaching budgeting, beat debt, and building legacy.

[13] C.f. www.DavidWilcox.com

life us in other ways. God may need to prepare us to be the right people to receive before giving us the winning ticket. *Following that illustration, how many lottery winners are dead broke and in considerable debt a year after winning millions of dollars?* These winners were not mentally or socially prepared to receive the winnings, so it all vanished. Sometimes the amount of time our investment is delayed in the field is because we need time to be molded us into someone who can handle His blessings. That is not a broken law, rather an education from a kind caring gracious investment banker. Dry periods require patience. However, the roots, our strength factor, grow more in-depth as we weather the dry seasons.

Without faith, it is impossible to please God. Coming to God requires believing that He genuinely exists and that He rewards those who diligently seek Him. -Hebrews 11:6

If my personal experience in investing didn't fulfill in a reasonable amount of time, I would examine whether I missed any critical steps in the process. My latest phone apps don't always work for me. I hand it to my son, who understands the entire process, and he returns it working correctly and instructs me in the proper preparation procedure. He has mastered the process. *The problem is usually operator error.* We must plant with intention, fertilize with joy, pray for the rain, work hard when the crop comes in, and reinvest some of the [whatever] with those who also need what we need. We must focus on a joyful attitude, as we must plant with a celebration in our hearts. We are in a shareholding partnership with God! Yes, God! Enjoy your position. Invest hard, you going to adore the view from your window one day.

<u>Second Intentional Investment Observation</u>
The attitude of our investment is a catalyst for our return, so invest with joy.

Chapter Three Conversation & Action

1. Would your spouse or closest friend describe you as a pessimist or an optimist?

2. Would your spouse or closest friend describe you as patient or impatient?

3. What sentence, paragraph, or idea from this chapter do you most want to talk about?

4. Find ways this week to practice joy in everything you do. Keep a log of your victories and your failures. Compare and consider how next week could be weighted more greatly toward the joy-filled side.

Chapter Four
See You at The Top

Shure Brothers[14] produce some of the most well-respected microphones in the world. In the earlier years of their audio dominance, they diversified their expertise into the world of audio mixers. They had great success with their small microphone mixers, and their 6 channel Vocal Master was a hit with churches and bar bands alike. In 1979 they unveiled the Pro Master 700 series microphone mixer. *I apologize for the technical details. I am confident the editors will remove most of what I penned to economize our word count.* Given the reputation of Shure Brothers, I ordered one. Assuredly, this machine was going to be the end-all mixer for my musical ventures. It might even get me signed to an impressive label. *Musicians lives are fueled by dreams.*

I remember the day the box arrived. We didn't have Youtube® back then, so I have no video footage to offer you showing my initial unboxing. *Pardon the sarcasm.* The mixer was beautiful and sounded better than expected. I built a road case for it, so I could take it on the road for my next tour. It was on that upcoming tour my Shure dream audio mixer decided to crash.

Upon calling my dealer, I was told to bring it back to Florida for a repair. Great, I am touring in Oklahoma, and you need me to bring it back to Florida so your service department can look at it for a while before they

---

[14] https://www.shure.com/en-US

decide to return it to the factory. They also informed me the service department was behind about two weeks.

I decided to take my situation to the source. I called Directory Assistance for the Shure Corporate number. For my younger readers, Directory Assistance was SIRI before SIRI was created. You dialed 411 on a large phone stoutly bolted to the wall in the kitchen and were connected with a person who had access every phone book in the world, and they looked up a number for you. Then you wrote it down on a piece of paper and dialed it on your rotary dial phone. If the phone number had a lot of nine's or zero's in it, our rotary phone could take quite a while just to dial it. If the line was busy, there was no call waiting, you impatiently started the process again.

Within minutes I was connected with the Shure Headquarters. After exchanging pleasantries with the receptionist, I asked to speak directly to one of the Shure Brothers. She laughed and responded, "Are you having a problem with one of our products?" I guess she had received this type of call before and she suggested I talk to a service representative. But I held fast, "If there is no Mr. Shure to speak to, I need you to put me through to the biggest big-wig in the company, the Grand-Poo-Bah, the El Jefe! I need to speak to the person who signs the checks." Within seconds I was speaking to the Vice President of Shure. I told him about my dilemma. Now this man did not know me from Adam, other than the fact I would have been the one wearing a more circa correct clothing choice. The Vice President took compassion on this young touring musician and responded, "Mr. Williams, we look at young musicians as our bread and butter. Where will you be in two days? I'm shipping a brand-new Pro Master mixer to your next tour location. Then when you have time, use the old shipping box to send me the broken one back using the included pre-paid return label. I believe I can trust you." Not only can they trust me, but they have made a Shure client for life.

Who is your source? Seriously, who is your ultimate source? Are you starting your request for advancement at some outsourced foreign call center, the HR Department, the mortgage banker, or are you reaching out to the origin of life itself? Are you planting in God's garden, or are you trying to scheme your way to the top? Intentional Investment is not a scheme, it is a God law. Join God's system.

Third Intentional Investment Observation
God is the Source of Our Harvest.

And God will generously respond with all you need. -2 Corinthians 9 v8a

Notice the verse declares God will be the one generously responding to you. This is bypassing the local dealer. This is avoiding Customer Service. This is going to the designer. I gave the money to the local dealer, but the creator was coming through for me.

The earth is the Lord's and the fullness of it... everything. -Psalms 24:1

Your source is not the bank, your source is not the grocer, your source is not a great aunt who has you in her will, whom you hope will pass on soon! When you know your source is you can express along with C.S. Lewis that, "Now you know the deeper magic."[15]

Re Sources

We refer to gifts, talents, love, money, seeds as our resources. They are [re]sources. They all came from the Source, our great God. We are granted the opportunity to [re]use them as we will. When we manage our [re]sources, seeing ourselves as being second in the chain of possession, it will change the way we invest, use, squander, or hoard them.

God is the instigator of our return on investment! Intentional investments are God-designed! This is God Gravity - it is a law written into the very fabric of the universe! Plant, water, harvest, eat some of the wheat, plant back some of the wheat, and the process goes on and on until you need a bigger truck or a bigger oven. *This is not an excuse for gluttony.*

God will supply everything we need according to His riches in Christ Jesus. - Philippians 4:19

If God is the source of our blessings, might He be willing to protect the blessings as well? The Source of your harvest is the Protector of your harvest. I am not

---

[15]

https://narnia.fandom.com/wiki/The_Deeper_Magic_from_Bef ore_the_Dawn_of_Time trusting my new video doorbell to show me videos of who took my stuff. I am not trusting my security system to call the police for me if I am not at home. I watch LivePD[16], and they never catch home invaders in the act. God is my source today, and my source tomorrow!

One plants the seed, another brings water to the plants, but God makes it grow. It's not the one who plants nor the one who waters who is at the center of this process. God makes things grow. Planting and watering are necessary. What makes the process worth the effort is the God we are serving. -1 Corinthians 3:6-9

Do I have a secret agenda? Some of you might be feeling this Intentional Investment narrative is actually a scheme to talk about tithing. Other readers may not even be familiar with the dreaded "T" word (tithe). Let's address the issue. For the sake of full understanding, let us remember the English word for the tithe word used in many of the Bible's financial investment narratives literally means giving a tenth. This goes back to Abraham's gift of ten percent (of his entire estate), given to the mysterious priest. The tithe process was repeated many times throughout the Old Testament, and one could find it in the New Testament as well. Biblical scholars understand the complete Hebrew tithes and offerings came much closer to twenty-six percent (26%) of their annual income. *I'm sure it was based on after-tax income and may have included health care.*

---

[16] https://www.aetv.com/shows/live-pd

Before you judge this book to be suggestively designed to inspire you to tithe more money to religious organizations, please hang on. You might have your disenchantment with the "tithe" word misaligned. This book is about something even more significant than money. *Don't you just love a mystery?*

If you do a google search for the "tithe" word, it will give you a loose modern translation about giving to a religious order or priest, and then proceed to define it away with the words "formerly given" to the church or a minister. *Let me give you a piece of advice; Never let Google, or Wikipedia, or even the Oxford online dictionary, be your source for biblical information.*

I dislike the word tithe as much as many. It is a boring word that should have received a makeover! *It sounds like an unwanted tax for a Congressional bridge to nowhere.* However, many [have chosen] to live in a financial tithing partnership with a church they are shareholders in. They are very comfortable doing that.

Every week I desire the opportunity to reinvest in successes. I see the church as an investment possibility too. When I visit other churches as a guest, I always invest in them too. In fact, when I put my pesos in the plate, I ask God to return it to me multiplied so I may use the harvest return for the good of His kingdom. Yes, I am very intentional.

Bring your investment into the storehouse, that the church may be well-stocked for service to the community. Let me show you how I will pour out

my heaven backed blessings, in a way that there will not be room enough to store it. I will prevent pests from eating your investments, and the vines in your fields will not drop their fruit before they are harvested ripe. Then all the nation will call you blessed, for your place of dwelling will be incredible. -Malachi 3:10-12

Giving, investing, tithing, and shareholding are not unpleasant words for someone who understands intentional investments. It is certainly not a scary word for those who have come to trust God. Let's be real honest. This book is not exclusively about money, but if you cannot trust your God with a portion of your rapidly depreciating currency, you certainly should not trust God with your eternity. You should start God-shopping and quick! *Check the internet, there are a lot of deity options there.*

The law works! The law is based on our planting, and God's return on our investment. However, as an ethical person, I desire to know I am investing in good soil. I genuinely want my investments to help other people as well as myself. My moral premise is foundational. This is why I don't give out money on street corners unless I specifically hear in my heart, God's voice screaming at me above the roar of religious radio. I am not swayed by the uncomfortable pressure of the guy holding his sign to my window. I trust he is not uncomfortable with me handing him directions to a local Rescue Mission my wife and I support. Yes, I want to know that every investment, even the small ones, make a significant difference.

Forget about dollars and cents! If you need higher education, plant the knowledge you have into someone else. If you need to be a better trombone player, find a horrible trombone player and help them sound decent. If you need friends - be a friend. If you need enemies - be an enemy! Kayaker, pianist, painter, mechanic, Whatever! It is a natural law, a reproducible reoccurring phenomenon! It is like gravity. Always remember your returned investment is coming from your God. A vertical source will respond to your horizontal needs.

The Golden Egg

In the 1970s L'eggs pantyhose were often packaged in large plastic reusable eggs in varied colors. Mothers and kids loved to repurpose them into toys and crafts. My mom always decorated these eggs for Resurrection Sunday morning. *I am told that a Resurrection Egg is different than an Easter Egg. I do hate to mix Christianity and paganism on such a special day.* She hid them around the yard for me to find. Notoriously, my mother would have one golden egg that was plastic and filled with dimes, nickels, and quarters. The golden one was my favorite egg to find. Did you ever hide resurrection eggs for children? Did the children ever miss seeing some of the eggs you hid even though they were right in front of them? Did you gently push them to return to their seeking until they found [all] the eggs? Did they fight you about going back to continue looking? Was their happiness restored when they finally found the treasured golden egg hiding right in front of their face?

The Treasured Rifle

My dad was a giving guy. He would give you the shirt off his back if he hadn't given it to someone else already that day. One day he called and joyfully told me about his plan. On our next family visit, he was going to ask my son (his grandson) to paint the shed for him. When my son finished painting, he would give him the hundred-year-old octagon barrel Stevens rifle that he had used to hunt squirrel in the 1930s. My son always loved that old gun. He asked me not to tell my son, as he wanted to surprise him. I agreed. Keep in mind this two-hour job required little more skill than moving your arms up and down. The problem was that my son was fifteen. *I don't know how old Isaac was when Abraham took him up the mountain to sacrifice him, but I'll bet he was fifteen.* At the age of fifteen, boys are not known for their desire to do much of anything other than sleep, and eat, and play video games. I saw a possible problem. I knew my father had a desire to bless my son, so I had to set my son up for success.

On the way over grandpa's house, I told my son that his grandfather was going to ask him to paint the shed and I expected him to do it without question. I didn't want to hear whining or complaining, and indeed no breath exhalation sounds. I wanted a joy-filled shed painting. I honored my father's request and kept the benefit a secret, but not the task. I did tell my son that while this would be a request from grandpa, this was a requirement from me. Later that day, when my son finished the painting task, he received the treasured family rifle. He was thrilled. He did not know that was the reward all along. If I had not laid down the law to my teenage son, his teenage laziness may have kicked in, and he might have found a teenage reason to avoid painting altogether. If he had never completed the required task, he would not have gained the rifle. Here was a requirement that turned out to be a great blessing.

What If God?

This is really important. What if the God of the Old Testament required his people to invest (tithe) for a reason? What if God had set up intentional investments to work for mankind from the first day of creation, but he had to force them to find it? Was required tithing God's way of pushing them to find their golden egg?

God required tithing in order to teach the people about His investment law, and to experience His prearranged ongoing blessings.

Have you ever had to push your child to do something in order to teach them a great truth? My father's secret rifle reward could be compared to God's predetermined - prearranged blessings resulting from our intentional investments. The treasured rifle is a representation of the harvest reward itself. Requiring my son to do the job with a happy attitude is parallel to Old Testament tithing. *If I were Jesus, I would say, "For those who have ears to hear, let them hear."*

Get to a point where you don't need to be forced to experience the blessings of planting and harvesting.

Let your mind wander back to our emotionally disturbing story of Elijah and the widow. Elijah pushed her into a decision. No question about it! Then he openly declared exactly where her continual supply of oil and bread mix would come from saying. "You shall have continued Bread mix and oil for your needs... thus says the Lord God of Israel." She gave to God through the conduit of her need, not her abundance. Her source was God.

Sometimes we need to be pushed to do the right thing. In doing the right thing, we experience great rewards. Sometimes we need to be forced to be a servant because if we do it with the right attitude, we will find someone serving us in our need. Sometimes we need to be pushed to do the right thing because if we do it with a good attitude, we will find the right deed being done for us. I want to get to the point where I don't need to be pushed. I want to joyfully live in the relaxed blessings of our God... planting and enjoying the harvest.

Third Intentional Investment Observation
God is the Source of Our Harvest.

Chapter Four Conversation & Action

1. Have you ever had to go past a customer service department to get something done?

2. What emotion does the "T" word stir in your mind?

3. Did you grow up in a religious tradition that taught tithing as a requirement or an option?

4. Have you ever required your child to do something to teach them a valuable life lesson?

5. What sentence, paragraph, or idea from this chapter do you most want to talk about?

6. Of the scripture verses listed in this chapter, which single scripture would be most beneficial to memorize?

7. Later this week, take time to consider how past misconceptions may have skewed the biblical principles you read today. Consider how false narratives or misunderstandings about stewardship (or tithing) may be keeping you from experiencing a greater blessing. Contemplate how legalism may have motivated or de-motivated your investments in whatever.

Chapter Five
Wait There's More

I love to play chess. I am not good at it, but I like to crush my opponent, even if my opponent is my eleven-year-old daughter. *It is a man thing.* Men are competitive in almost anything we do. I'm not saying it is right. Have you ever played 3-Dimensional chess? It has different playing pieces on one of three separate interactive glass playing levels. You have to simultaneously keep up with what is going on above you and below you.

> *For every action there is an equal*
> *and opposite reaction. -Isaac Newton*

God is a chess player who always plays on seven billion interactive glass playing levels.[17] If we could envision them all, I am sure our heads would explode. Humans tend to process on one level... our small piece of the earth. However, what we do on our small piece of Earth affects things in Heaven. Things in Heaven direct our life, our family, and our children here on Earth. Our life lived today, alters our life tomorrow. Every action causes another action or response.

Fourth Intentional Investment Observation
There are eternal rewards for our investments.

Invest and you will always have abundance, and
plenty left over to share with others. As the

---

[17] Estimated Earth population circa 2019 at 7 billion

Psalmist wrote, "They share freely and give generously to the poor. Their good deeds will be remembered forever." -2 Corinthians 9 v8b-9

Among the Israelite farming community, was the religious requirement to leave the outside edges of their crops unharvested, and freely available for the hungry traveler passing their farm.[18] It was their ongoing intentional investment in feeding the hungry. When choosing in faith to leave a portion of their harvest to feed others, they received a higher harvest yield in the next season. *Sounds like a secret life-hack to me.*

So maybe I should leave a little for others as an investment. After an earlier chapter's slightly harsh critique of sign-carrying panhandlers, you may choose to call me hypocritical. Let me explain that my wife prepares reusable grocery bags. She fills them with a toothbrush, toothpaste, shampoo, a small hand towel, a bar of soap, a light blanket, a few granola bars, Christian literature, and information about our local Lighthouse Rescue Mission. She keeps these bags in her car. On the occasions she feels spiritually moved to engage with a panhandler, she blesses them with a bag of real necessities. The bags are not given to everyone. Only those few whom she feels God specifically leading her to invest in. She listens to God in her heart. It is also a great way to teach our children about generosity. *Don't everybody do this, or they will all have to have carts to carry the bags, and they will never go to the Rescue Missions for real help.*

---

[18] Leviticus 23:22

Plant your investment of tithes and offerings... I will prevent pests from eating your investments, and the vines in your fields will not drop their fruit before they are harvested ripe. -Malachi 3:10-12

Not only is there short-term protection and reward for our investment, but for the children of God, there is extremely long-term return on our investment. Beyond our salvation, as we saw in a previous chapter, we will be rewarded in eternity for our life investments.

God is not unjust. He is not forgetful. He would never forget your continued work and labor of love... -Hebrews 6:10a

We are reminded [again] in Paul's correspondence to the Hebrews, how God will bless our lives in response to our [work] and [labors of love]. Generosity will be rewarded with generosity, refreshment will be rewarded with refreshment, and love will bring more love. Plant your single kernel of corn, you are going to enjoy a big bag of corn. *I hope you all love corn.* It's the law.

There are a few really troublesome verses for me as a modern-day "grace" over "law" guy. These harsh verses come to us from the very vocal cords of Jesus the Christ. *We are talking red letters here.* Matthew records Jesus as declaring how it would be at the end of time.[19] Jesus separates all the people of the world by their charitable investments (monetary and/or non-

---

[19] Matthew 25:31-46

monetary). He says to the faithful and [righteous] investors, "I was hungry, and you fed me, I was naked, and you clothed me, I was in prison and you visited me, I was sick and you brought me the medicine." The [righteous] investors respond, "When did we serve you in this manner?" Jesus responds, "When you invested in the least of these, you invested in me. Enter now into the ultimate reward for your investment… eternity in heaven."

In this narrative, the [righteous] people were [not] being charitable for the sole purpose of inheriting a heavenly condo. It does not appear they realized they were giving to Jesus and investing in their future when they were giving to the needy. Possibly their only thought of blessing was what would come as an earthly reward. I am not trying to create a new doctrine here. Nevertheless, this is biblical narrative.

Jesus split the story turning to the unrighteous group with some devastating words saying, "I was hungry, and you gave me nothing, I was naked, and you brought me no clothing, I was in prison, and you drove past, I was sick, and you brought no medicine." Ouch! These are certainly not the most grace-filled words we have ever heard from Jesus. *I have never seen this kind of presentation this side of those scary little Chick Publication booklets.* "The [unrighteous non-investors] respond, "When did we not do good to you?" Jesus responds, "When you failed to invest in the least of these, you failed to invest in me. Go to hell!" Was the last line too harsh for you? Well, it is what He stated. *Take it up with Jesus.*

Recapping, Jesus declared internally righteous people invest in the needs of others and will be rewarded in eternity. Unrighteous people do not invest in others and receive a pretty stout boot kick to a devil's dog house. I'm not going to try and reconcile the verse to our modern-day grace theology. I'm just laying it out for your consideration. *Some of us will choose to grab a bicycle and hope the forgiveness prayer line is working every day!*

> **Feeding others, was feeding Jesus.**
> **Clothing others was clothing Jesus.**
> **Caring for others was caring for Jesus.**
> **Visiting others was visiting Jesus.**
> **All of it was an investment in eternity.**

My wife and I are deeply connected to the Crossover Cups mission in the Dominican Republic.[20] Many of our activities involve the feeding of a large group of children who live from a garbage dump. I remember the first day we drove into a fly-infested burning trash deposit. It was the day God spoke to our hearts, "FEED THESE PEOPLE IN MY NAME!" We didn't know how we would do it and certainly did not know how we could afford it. We did not pray for God to send somebody there to do what He was calling us to do.

The [failure] of prayer is not in speaking but in listening. We tell God about needs as if He was unaware of the needs. *Personally, I would not want to worship an*

---

[20] www.CupsMission.com

unaware God. We give him our list of desires and give Him some wimpy ideas of how He might respond to our list. After years of seeing no response, we quit praying. Very understandable is the sequence here. If prayer doesn't work; why pray? How different could it be if we phrased our prayers with serious and personal questions? What if we took the He is the head, and we are the hands and feet seriously? We would pray differently. We would not give God suggestions. We would articulate situations and ask Him what we were to do about it, or how we were to respond to it. Then our action would bring the God-ordained response. Pray that way, and you will see your prayers answered.[21]

Only one life will soon be passed. Only what is done for Christ will last. -C.T. Studd[22]

God placed an excellent investment opportunity in a fly infested garbage heap. What would we do? We started feeding people there. We started feeding Jesus there! Now, with the help of others around the country, these poor people are being fed five days a week. Because of the investment of others, there is a discipleship center for them, and their children are in an education program so one day they will not have to live in the garbage dump. Join us one day as we feed there. I will bet you feel the hand of God on yours. Walk with us on the burning trash pile of hell called the Sosua Garbage dump and feel His pleasure with your

---

[21] A greater understanding of this prayer concept can be found in the book entitled Shut Up, Get in the Jeep, and Let Me Drive by Mike & Terica Williams.

[22] C.f. www.goodreads.com/author/quotes/3441241.C_T_Studd

investment. I know if there is one thing I have done of enduring and eternal value; it has been investing in God's most impoverished children. The mission was a leap of faith. Nevertheless, it has become for us a proof of the reality of God.

Faith without action is lifeless, without any value, not really even faith. -James 2:17

Joy-filled intentional investing goes way beyond money ever will! I cannot tell you of a day we have ever gone to our own pantry and found it empty. *When we invest in God's law, he provides our crop duster, our worm killer, and our scarecrow!* He stands guard over our investment. Let me again stress to you our investment protection is for finance, and talent, and giftedness, and knowledge, and so on. *Whatever!*

The old colloquialism articulates that you get what you pay for. God's Law of Intentional Investment says you harvest more than you planted into the ground, more than you planted into others, more than you gave into service, and more than you invested into the offering. Do you desire more?

<u>Fourth Intentional Investment Observation</u>
There are eternal rewards for our investments.

Chapter Five Conversation & Action

1. Share some alternative ways to minister to panhandlers.

2. Have you ever been on a third-world mission trip?

3. Who benefited more from the mission trip, you or the people you served?

4. What sentence, paragraph, or idea from this chapter do you most want to talk about?

5. Of the scripture verses listed in this chapter, which single scripture would be most beneficial to memorize?

6. During your next personal devotion time, consider what an evaluation of your life investments would say about your faith, and your personal consecration to the Father. If faith without works is dead, contemplate the trues vitality of your faith.

Chapter Six
Cats Make More Cats

Have you ever wanted to be a great guitar player? I love guitars. The acoustic guitar has always carried a special place in my heart and ear. I love the way you can strum it like a harp while beating it like a drum. I love the harmonics you experience as each string cuts through the mix of melody and harmony. I love the way it feels in my hands. I appreciate the way it sounds, so unlike the German accordion, my parents forced me to learn when I was nine. My children will tell you if I am not typing on the computer, I most likely have small hand-crafted carbon-fiber parlor guitar in my hand. I play along with every television show theme song, and jam with every musical performance on Austin City Limits. I even join on the commercials jingles. *Nationwide® is on your side.*

I am not the best guitar player in the world, but I can hold my own. If you saw me in concert, you might believe I was somewhat an expert. I know a lot of cool guitar hacks, and I can loop and tap with pretty good articulation. Ask me how I became the guitarist I am and I will not tell you it was [not] my six weeks of lessons. It was not Paul Frampton (Peter's cousin) who gave me my first good acoustic guitar. It was not Youtube guitar teachers, for we did not even have computers back then. The secret to my guitar prowess started when I began to take the little I knew about the guitar, and planted it into others who knew even less. As I invested what I knew, I knew what I knew better.

Beyond the talent improvement, at fourteen years old, I [invested] through playing at nursing homes to people who were barely awake and often drooling. My minimal ability increased as I gave away my ability to those seniors. *I have now played for single crowds as large as eighty-thousand people. Less of them were asleep or drooling than in the early years.* At fourteen, this life-hack of intentional investment concept alluded me. Although I did not understand this law, my musical investment would come back to bless me over and over again.

Fifth Intentional Investment Observation
Plant Intentionally What You Desire To Harvest.

For God is the one who provides seed for the farmer that becomes his bread. In the same way, God will provide and increase your resources.
-2 Corinthians 9:10

In the same way... God will provide. It starts with your resources - planted! Whatever you intentionally plant - you will reap in direct correlation (type) to whatever you planted. Planting yellow corn does not deliver a crop of green apples or purple sugar beets. It produces more yellow corn.

Let the earth bring forth living creatures that shall reproduce similar living creatures. -Genesis 1:24

From the beginning, God has been reproducing animals, talents, gifts, everything... after their own kind. Please push away from the obvious financial ramifications. Let's keep it a little less monetary for a minute or two.

Do you desire to be a better writer? Intentionally teach someone who is a worse writer than you how to be a better writer. In doing so, you will become a better writer. It's the law. *In fact, help me with my next book!*

Do you desire to be a better pilot? Then you should Intentionally mentor someone who is a worse pilot than you how to be a better pilot. In doing so, you will become a better pilot. It's the law. *You might first teach a worse pilot in a simulator rather than in the actual air. Think safety people!*

Do you desire to be a better teacher? Intentionally mentor in a less skilled teacher. It's the law.

Do you desire to be a better baker? Intentionally mentor a younger baker. It's the law.

Do you desire to be a better mom? Intentionally mentor a younger mom. It's the law.

Do you desire to be a better carpenter? Intentionally mentor a new carpenter. It's the law.

Pardon the repetition... get over it. Let's get very personal.

Fill in the blank with a need of your own:

"Heavenly Father, I desire to be a better
_____. Thus, I have joyfully
determined to find someone who is weaker in that area
than myself and intentionally invest in their
improvement. In return, I expectantly await your Law
of Intentional Investment to thrive in my own life.
Amen!"

Throughout recordable history, each species
reproduced from their own DNA bank. Naturally, seeds
would do the same. If you need money, plant money. If
you need tomatoes, Plant tomatoes. By the way, if you
need people to be angry at you, shout angrily at them.
It's the law.

Farming is complicated. If you plant tomatoes,
you are not going to harvest fried chicken.
Who knew? But that would be cool too.

Let's bring greater understanding to the word
intentional. You don't plant tomatoes and expect to
harvest shoes. Intentional, deliberate investments take
account of what we intentionally desire to receive. What
do you need? How could you plant in a parallel manner?
Do you need shoes? Do you need food? Do you need
Knowledge? Do you need cooking lessons? *The cook last
week at Denny's sure did.* Invest in specific areas where you
need to receive. We often confuse the need for money
as an answer to all needs. Often paper money is merely
an alternative representative. *When you can't send a goat
through the mail, you send money to buy a goat.*

With stones, Elijah built an altar in the name of the Lord his God. He added a large seed trench around the altar. The wood was well placed, a fuel that with the help of heavenly fire would reduce his valuable offering to worthless ashes. He cut the bull into pieces and laid it on the altar. Though in short supply, Elijah called for twelve barrels of precious water to be poured onto the sacrifice, and to fill the seed trench. The water ran throughout the bull pieces, the wood, and completely filled the seed trench.
-1 Kings 18:32-35

I know a guy who is a Generosity Coach. His formal title is Pastor Zach Terry.[23] He illuminated the following Elijah story to me one Sunday after a special sermon on generosity. I am betting that you have never heard this story before with these interesting observations. I had not.

Once upon a time, there was drought in the land.[24] No rain had fallen for a really long time. No rain meant no water for the people or their flocks. Their crops were shriveling in the field from lack of water. Elijah, God's prophet, challenged the false prophets to a fire-making God proving duel. The winning God would most certainly be able to make it rain for the people as a nice consolation prize for any prophets killed as part of the show. The crowd gathered, and Jezebel's prophets came dressed in black, their team

---

[23] www.ZachTerry.com/
[24] C.f. 1 Kings 18:17-46

shirts number 1 to 450 consecutively. They created a delightful altar. They brought in a really nice bull to be an unwilling part of the festivities. Music filled the air as they chanted their chants, played their tambourines and accordions, shouted, and even cut themselves for hours. Between the bull butchering and the prophets cutting, it was a bloody mess. You certainly could not call them apathetic in their attempt. Sadly for them, no fire came. Apparently, their God was dead. *No forthcoming movie is being planned.* Their altar was lovely, their production well-choreographed, and I'd give it a 7. But their sacrifice had no grand finale! The bull stunk, the land was still dry, and the skies were still cloudless. *No umbrella sales today.*

Then Elijah stepped up and built a very similar altar, adding nothing but a large [seed-holding] trench. He used one of the same two bulls brought in for the other prophets. Adding only one item to his sacrifice, he added that which is needed the most in times of drought, he added water. In fact, he took Twelve barrels of water from their quickly diminishing supply. This water could have hydrated the few remaining cattle and the people as well. Think about this for a minute. Elijah invested (sacrificed) precisely the item the people needed the most... water. He placed it in a [seed] trench. Interesting choice of words, don't you think? BAM! We have already discovered that Elijah was a prophet that understood intentional investments.

Elijah sang, I've seen fire and I've seen rain long before James Taylor.

Have you read the story before? God sent fire from heaven and consumed the sacrifice... including the water... and then the rain came. Can you see a parallel in this story to our intentional investing narrative? If not, maybe you need to go back to Kindergarten. *I'm serious.* If it were me, I would have added a little gasoline to the offering too, just to help God out. *That is the way I roll.* Hey friends, what are you putting in your seed trench?

Seeds of Proof

On September 22, 1940, Perry Hayden said, "I am going to take God at his word and see what happens." He pledged to inspire the world and prove that the law of intentional investment (the tithe) worked in every (whatever) area of their life - not only money. He did this by taking one square inch of wheat, not much bigger than a sugar cube, and planting each tiny individual seed by hand in twelve rows. He committed to tithe ten percent of the forthcoming crop and sow the remaining seeds again. The [essential] ten percent (tithe) removed from each harvest was sold, and used to support church projects (and eventually build hospitals). His next incoming crop was too large for the land he owned. Intrigued by the experiment, auto maker Henry Ford came along to provide the land needed to re-plant the growing seed stock from each previous year. In six years, that project grew to a staggering figure that can be read about in the history books. At their average rate of growth, they would have been able to cover the entire United States of America with wheat in less than twenty years. It all started with a commitment to intentionally invest a single square inch of wheat and give away ten percent of the increase. Henry Ford, amid this tremendous *Dynamic Kernels Wheat Project,* proclaimed that "My experiments in tithing may well eclipse anything else I have done in my lifetime." That is quite a statement coming from the man who gave the common man the automobile and is often credited with launching the industrial revolution.[25]

Stop continually looking for money! Get specific. If I believed I needed a pair of shoes today, I might find a good pair in my closet and share them with a homeless family or a third world mission. Then I would wait for God to grow my shoe investment. Of course, I pray. Prayer is a conversation. I might even thank God in advance. Some of you are shaking your head in disbelief. All I can do is tell you what has happened to me and my friends.

<u>Fifth Intentional Investment Observation</u>
Plant Intentionally What You Desire To Harvest.

Chapter Six Conversation & Action

1. Did you ever plant any seeds?

2. Did the seeds produce what you planted?

3. What is your favorite hobby?

---

[25] https://www.youtube.com/watch?v=-EP2qrQf5p0

4. Who taught you the most about that hobby?

5. Have you ever taught someone your skill or hobby?

6. Did both of your benefit from the training?

7. What sentence, paragraph, or idea from this chapter do you most want to talk about?

8. Of the scripture verses listed in this chapter, which single scripture would be most beneficial to memorize?

9. In your spare time, find *Dynamic Kernels Wheat Project* on Youtube and watch it.

Chapter Seven
Good For The Heart

At this point, one might cogitate your author is a greedy man. Anyone who could spend six chapters talking about betterment, harvest, increase, and money must need a little pastoral financial counseling. Does your author have a greed problem? Let me be perfectly clear. I find the overtly consumeristic mentality of my culture to be rather disturbing, though I do own a Mac. On the other hand, when living in the Dominican Republic, my family and I live in a 484 square foot two-room house, that has no hot water and no air condition. I would love to be featured on Tiny House Nation.[26]

More – More – More!

Have you ever watched the television show Hoarders? A team of cleaners, garbage men, and a psychologist enter the home of someone who has collected so much junk they can barely walk into the house anymore. Some can't walk in at all. The hoarder is literally up to their roof in the garbage (treasures to them). Most of these people started collecting for what they felt was a good reason. Their reasons range from not wanting to watch perfectly good items thrown away, to collecting for the end of the world when Jesus comes back. *Apparently, when Jesus returns, He is not bringing enough food, clothing, old newspapers, animal feces, or expired food with Him.* Some started collecting with the thought of giving things away to people in need, but they became

---

[26] https://www.fyi.tv/shows/tiny-house-nation?newexp=true

obsessed with their collection. At some point, the collection started collecting them. *I'm just saying a person does not need over five-hundred porcelain dolls no matter how much they remind them of a second cousin who resembles Jimmy Fallon.* Hoarding on any level is wrong. Maybe this will be the gluttony chapter.

When we desire to receive a compounded return on our investment, it has nothing to do with greed. Giving love and receiving more love in return doesn't sound greedy. Providing hope and receiving more hope in return doesn't seem greedy. Giving away our knowledge and gaining more expertise does not sound greedy. But again, bring the money into it and all of the sudden people get their spiritual goat up! Why? Is the gold ore and silver ore that God created dastardlier than iron ore? Gold and silver may have paid for the workers of the world, but the iron ore built the buildings securing it. Some ignorantly believe the Bible declares all money to be filthy lucre.

Staple shut the mouth of those who corrupt the truth for filthy lucre's sake. -Titus 1:11

The biblical term "filthy lucre" is not given to [all] monetary exchanges. Our filthy lucre term was only assigned to the financial gain obtained through false teaching, greed, or deceptive teaching. When we bring our monetary investments to the Lord, we are not bringing Him filthy lucre, we bring Him a holy financial investment.

Take leadership and feed the people of God around you. Don't use force. Don't do it for a paycheck of filthy lucre. Don't have ulterior motives. Don't be a dictator over God's heritage. Be an example to all people. Do this well, and when the chief Shepherd Jesus shall finally appear, you will receive a permanent crown of glory. -1 Peter 5:2-4

Pay attention here. Our 1 Peter reference makes no argument with the leader [receiving] a crown of glory. God is not against rewarding individual persons! God, the only great good perfect being is somehow willing to reward humankind for our [micro] goodness amid our [major] imperfection. God has always rewarded those who passionately seek Him. He also allows it to rain upon the good and the bad. *And rain can be good, or rain can be bad.* God is a rewarder!

And without faith it is impossible to please God, because anyone who comes to him must believe that he exists and that he rewards those who earnestly seek him. -Hebrews 11:6 *NIV*

Personally… I give - to receive! *That is how I roll! That is how I hack!* But wait there's more. I give - to receive - to give again. We can righteously and wisely use the law of God's return on investment, as long as we don't become a hoarder. So, give - to receive - to give again. As followers of Christ, we give - to receive - to give - to receive - to give - to receive - to give - to receive - to give. We always end with the generosity and desire to give more. We can safely participate because we can't out-give God's provisional warehouse. While we were hopeless sinners, God gave Jesus! *That is a BIG GIVE!* And He keeps giving.

Put on your theology cap for a short foray. Did not the cross of Christ, the death of one, and the resurrection of one, become the redemption harvest of many? Did Caiaphas[27] subliminally comprehend the sowing and reaping nature of God in recommending that one should die for all the people. His statement was pure truth. Jesus reminded us that one seed of wheat falls must fall to the ground and die so that much fruit can come of it.[28] Let's not get off track here. I just found the parallel interesting. Thanks for chasing the rabbit with me.

<u>Sixth Intentional Investment Observation</u>
Intentional Investors Have A Generous Heart.

God will continue to produce a great harvest of generosity in you. Yes, you will be enriched in every way so that you can always be generous.
-2 Corinthians 9:10b-11

Sometimes ignorance of the whole scripture can be confused with devoutness. I can almost hear some humble soul saying, "I just want whatever God wants. I don't want to be pushy or greedy. I don't need filthy lucre. I will just wait on the Lord for His blessings. Whatever the Lord wants - I want. I will remain

---

[27] John 18:14
[28] John 12:24

humble." It certainly sounds holy and pious. *Pronouncing humble with a silent 'h' makes you look even more humble.* God set up everything in His creation, including your very life to start with the smallest seed and grow into something bigger and better. Will you move with His plan or will you wallow in self-proclaimed humility and call it spirituality?

Failure to utilize the productively favorable laws of God are as unspiritual as breaking admonitory laws of God. Living out the Law of Intentional Investment is not about greed. It is about taking God-given advantage for the sake of God's kingdom made visible on earth. It is about abundant life today, as well as tomorrow. Some of our beloved membership has become so enamored with heaven, they forgot about those who might outlive them on this earth. This investment life hack definitely impacts our eternal future, but it does not in any way underplay our role to bring about the kingdom of God on earth. *You can sing I'll Fly Away without adding a verse that throws flaming napalm out of the window of your departing heavenly hearse.*

Intentional Investment is not about greed. It is about our God-given ability to be intentionally generous and decidedly gracious!

I am told of a man who fell from the side of a cliff. He is clinging to one lonely branch protruding from the rock. *I'm sure the tree branch was placed there for the sake of our story.* Our devoutly spiritual and very religious man cries out for God to save him. Seconds later an Atheist in a helicopter passes overhead and drops a ladder to the man, but our devout friend waves if off, choosing to be a man of faith. "I will wait on God to rescue me," he shouts. Seconds later he hears the voices of a long-haired traveling rock band above him and sees a microphone cable coming over the side of the cliff. Obviously, our devoutly religious cliff clinger refused the cable saying, "NO, I am waiting on God to rescue me." The devout man eventually loses his strength and experiences God's law of gravity. *It was not pretty.* Splat! Waking up in heaven, shaken and disturbed, he asks why God did not rescue him. God responds, "I sent a helicopter and a band with cable, and you rejected them each time. In emergency situations, I work through the nearest people, whether they be rock bands or atheists."

Blessings come through various channels.

Apathy is not spiritual! Lethargy is not spiritual! Procrastination is not spiritual! When we reject the Laws of God, we are rejecting the help of God. When we refuse to use the resources God has preordained, we are demonstrating confidence in ourselves more than belief in Him. Make no mistake about it, joyful intentional investing requires an enormous trust factor… at first. Greater trust is needed as we invest more significant amounts of love, time, or money. Sometimes it is easier to trust God with monetary investments than it is to trust Him with time investments. Time is what I seem to have the least of.

It is as greedy to reject the resources of God as it is greedy to abuse those resources.

Greediness is not having remarkable possessions. Greediness is hoarding the possessions you have. You can be greedy with a little as much as you can be greedy with a lot! How we use the Law of Intentional Investment is totally up to us. We must guard our hearts against becoming greedy. There is no place for greed in the heavenly or earthly kingdom of God.

Jesus warned, "Watch out! Guard against all kinds of greediness. The value of a man's life is not verified by the toys in his garage or garages." -Luke 12:15

Nevertheless, some people use the laws of God to receive significant gain. God's laws work, whether you are a Christ-follower or not. A secular person can experience God's creation of gravity. An unregenerate person can experience God's creation of oxygen. A sinner can experience God's creation of harvest. If God's [harvest] does not discriminate as to individual persons, there is always a high chance of misuse, yet the law is not negated! God does not withhold rain because it blesses people who are not believers.

…the thieves, the greedy, the drunkards, the slanderers, the swindlers will not inherit the kingdom of God. -1 Corinthians 6:10

The greedy often search for happiness in items, objects, houses, wealth, sex, or power. Greed does not fulfill our need for God. It only fills the time we have been given to find a genuine relationship with God.

Investing is not greedy. Jesus seemed to see investing as a matter of life or death.

Jesus declared, "You wicked and slothful servant! You ought to have invested my money with the bankers, and at my coming, I should have received what was my own with interest. So take the talent from him and give it to him who has gained ten talents. For everyone who has will more be given, and he will have an abundance. But from the one who has not, even what he has will be taken away. Cast the worthless servant into the outer darkness. In that place, there will be weeping and gnashing of teeth."
-Matthew 25:26-30 ESV

Ouch! One translation refers to the non-investing servant as lazy. It doesn't end with pink ponies, happy thoughts, and strawberry cake for this non-investor. Jesus stipulated; the property owner wanted an increase from each tenant. Was this story for real or just a filler parable? *If we hold hands and chant, "Bicycle... bicycle...bicycle," maybe that parable will disappear.* Stay with me, please.

End with Generosity

We do not give only to receive. Receiving and keeping can be dangerous. We give - to receive - to give again! We always end with generosity. We desire to obtain a great harvest so we can significantly bless others. We want to give love so we can receive so much love that we can do nothing more than give love away in bundles. What about you? *GIVE BIG!*

Sixth Intentional Investment Observation
Intentional Investors Have A Generous Heart.

———————————

Chapter Seven Conversation & Action

1. Could your closet or garage be featured on a television show about hoarders?

2. Describe the difference between greedy and thrifty?

3. Describe the difference between greedy and generous?

4. Define the word stewardship?

5. Why is the parable of the unfaithful servant uncomfortable to talk about?

6. What sentence, paragraph, or idea from this chapter do you most want to talk about?

7. Of the scripture verses listed in this chapter, which single scripture would be most beneficial to memorize?

8. Think of someone who could benefit from
    something that you could provide. Do
    something about that.

Chapter Eight
Bonus Reward Cards

I watch commercials as much as I watch television shows. Commercials pay for programming. They don't film a thirteen-week sitcom because it's simple, fun, and cheap to do in their spare time. It is all about advertising dollars. I love commercials. *Because of commercials, I know Arby's has the beef!*

I much appreciate the insurance commercials and their engaging stories running from week to week. I look forward to anything new from the English brogue of the Geico Gecko, the latest antics of Flo and Jamie over at Progressive, and I certainly need to eye what craziness Farmers has insured this week and memorialized in their Accident Hall of Fame.

I also love the Cash Back Bonus Rewards Card commercial. These people know how to create a title. It says it all. This card gives me 1. Cashback, 2. Bonuses, and 3. Rewards. Give me all three of those.

An Investment that Gives Back

According to the Apostle Paul, the Law of Intentional Investment works in much the same way. We can receive bonus investment points! It is time we discovered the Heavenly Rewards Card! *Sign me up!*

<u>Seventh Intentional Investment Observation</u>
There Are Added Bonus Rewards.

And when we take your gifts to those who need them, they will thank God. Two good things will result from this ministry of giving. The needs of the believers will be met, and they will joyfully express their thanks to God. Because of your sharing, they will give glory to God for your generosity to them. This proves we are obedient to the Good News of Christ. And they will pray for you with deep affection because of the overflowing grace God has given to you. Thank God for this gift that is too wonderful for words!
-2 Corinthians 9:11b-14

Wow! Thank God for His Law of Intentional Investments! Look closely at 2 Corinthians 9:12a. The first of our bonus points extend to a deep need inside all of our souls. It is why the very title alone of the bestseller The Purpose Driven Life[29] caused many of us to read it. Inside each of us is the need to have a purpose. We all wonder [why] we are here. We desire to know we [genuinely] made a difference. I certainly do. I want to know I did more than suck oxygen from this planet. *Can I be at least a minor superhero for somebody?*

Stephen Hawking[30] is often touted as having the most brilliant scientific mind of recent generations. Some say that his wheelchair and electronic talking machine highly favor his intrigue and notoriety. Nevertheless, his intellectual prowess has impacted many theories of the universe, most of them unprovable

---

[29] http://purposedriven.com/books/pdlbook/
[30] https://en.wikipedia.org/wiki/Stephen_Hawking

at this point in history. "Why are we here?" is his most famous question. With all of his theoretical answers, Hawking has repeatedly asked this question. Stephen cannot answer the question fully without allowing for a [creator] to exist. *It must be tough to be a scientist who is unwilling to look at all possible answers.* I believe that the Creator placed in the DNA of every person, first a desire to know the Creator, and secondly to have a life-giving purpose ourselves. If we are created in His image, we would naturally desire to do what He does.

I desire to live a life more worthy of a statue than a tombstone!

I have for many years, been contracted by churches and para-church organizations to speak at their major fundraising events. *Apparently, comedy inspires people give generously. These organizations have compensated me well for bringing the hilarity to the charity.* My clients usually schedule hours to tell me about their needs so I can reiterate those needs with the audience. I often cut them short. I remind them people don't care what they need, in comparison to what problem they successfully solve. People desire to be a part of a victory. Their success story is not that they are here, but rather that they are doing a great job fixing a genuine problem. That is the subconscious driver behind our willingness to invest.

Who wants to be a winner?

I won't give to (invest) in a losing cause, even if you attach the word "Christian" to it. Connecting the "C" word does not make something spiritual or even necessary. People often [abuse] the "C" word, making it into a blazing stamp of mediocrity. I would rather see a loving genuine action-filled follower of Christ, than see a shirt with a hip cross or a catchy religious slogan emblazoned on it. You dig?

> ***Purposeful intentional investing demands
> we have a clear concept of what
> our gift will accomplish.***

As for the financial offerings, partnerships, and investment opportunities in our church collection plates, the leadership has the responsibility to present the offering times with a clear understanding of the needs. They need to share how that need will be rectified because of our investment. Tell me about the results! As American citizens and Christians, you and I have the right to invest or not invest, and do that in whatever donation plate, program, or purpose we choose. We all have choices. It would behoove our churches to let us know their mission plan. Within our hearts is a desire to live in a way that brings success to our world story. We all desire purpose and personal significance. For me, not every investment gift is about a reciprocal blessing of talent, or time, or money. I often give for the sheer deep-down satisfaction of knowing that I made a difference. That significance alone can't be bought for any amount of money. I want to leave a legacy.

When it comes to your investment in the local church, help your church leadership understand what motivates you and others to invest. Church leadership should treat the church financial request time with information and expectation. This is not 1957 or 1972. Shareholders (you and I) want to know what need is being met with our investment. If leadership doesn't [inspire] the audience with transformations, the shareholders will dwindle. Welcome to the real world of church partnership. Church leadership needs to know how to inspire a congregation to invest. Might I suggest that you expose your leaders to the instructional manual for Pastors entitled Cultivating A Generous Congregation.[31]

I know a man who recently left his board position at a critical denominationally backed ministry because they had spent five million dollars and had not one single trafficked girl they could show as being transformed. I understand. People need to be part of something great. Results are essential to the investor. Wise investors seek good soil. Church and para-church ministries need to be good soil. If you can't trust the soil in your present house of worship, go to a place where you can. Invest joyfully with great expectation in your local church with time, and talent, and finances! Over the years the local church has proven to be a great God investment bank.

A greater inspection of 2 Corinthians 9:12b-13 declares that God receives thanksgiving and [glory] from our giving, and it proves we are [obedient] to the good news of Christ. What is the good news of Christ?

---

[31] Amazon.com see Cultivating A Generous Congregation Renovate Publishing

Is it forgiveness? Is it eternal life? Is it abundant life? What would you say? The good news of Christ is pretty far-reaching. *If you watched the A&E Life of Christ special, you already know this.* Let's listen to what Jesus [the Christ] himself declared He was here to do.

Jesus declared, "The Spirit of the Lord is upon me, because he has anointed me to proclaim good news to the poor. He has sent me to proclaim liberty to the captives, and recovery of sight to the blind, to set at liberty those who are oppressed, to proclaim the year of the Lord's favor." -Luke 4:18-19

Look at the [fullness] of the good news. Abundant life is for everyone! The poor receive equal access - they are not invisible to God or God's partners. Those in bondage receive what they have been praying for - freedom from their shackles. The blind - experience the sight of a beautiful day. The oppressed - receive justice and fairness. And finally, we are in a place where we detect God's favor on us. What does the word "favor" mean to you? What could [God's favor] include?

Jesus said, "The enemy has come to kill, steal, and destroy. I have come that they might have life, and have that life in greater abundance." -John 10:10b

Jesus is clearly talking about abundant life in the here and now, not only eternity. The blessings of God [are] for eternity, but they are also for today and tomorrow. God wants you to experience the best life you can. He wants you to enjoy life on this earth and enjoy Him forever. Jesus taught us to pray for God's kingdom to come to earth as well.

And they will pray for you with deep affection because of the overflowing grace God has given to you. -2 Corinthians 9:14

Do you really believe in prayer? Return to our foundational scriptures and dig deep into the prayer factor of 2 Corinthians 9:14. Personally, I don't know how prayer works. Neither do I understand gravity. I do believe prayer causes things to happen that would not happen otherwise. A residual blessing from our generosity, our sharing, our loving, our encouraging, our planting, and our investments, is that the human recipients of those blessings will call out our names to God. Wow! We are not talking about the casual "God bless you" lines we give and don't remember past the next minute. The Bible says these people will [PRAY] for us with [fervor] and [passion] and deep affection.

There is a missionary pastor friend my family has supported for many years. I know he prays for us with deep affection. Nights he did not know I was in the most dangerous place in my life, God woke him up to pray for me. Our occasional financial investment partnership with him might cause a little extra prayer to be coming our way. *That is honesty, and it is okay....Amen! I will take all the prayer I can get.*

DANIEL'S PIGGY BANK

Daniel's church had a special missionary offering one Sunday. Instead of passing the offering plate, they decided to have people come forward to place their offering in the silver plates on the communion table. People filed forward and put their investments in the collection plates. The last person at the table was this little nine-year-old boy struggling to maintain his grip on a giant piggy bank. Yes, nine-year-old Daniel had brought his piggy bank down the aisle rattling with change all the way.

Daniel was blind to the attention, but every eye was watching him. People were chuckling, smiling, and even taking photos as they watched the young boy. When he arrived at the front, he pulled the rubber plug from the underside of the pig and began to shake it mightily as the coins fell out and hit the table. Some rolled onto the floor; some into the offering plate. Wanting to be sure the piggy bank was empty, he lifted it high in the air and stuck his finger inside to pull out the paper money and began to throw the crumpled bills into the collection plate. When he was assured it was empty, he put the stopper back in the piggy bank and turned to make his way back to his seat with his mom and dad.

The pastor stopped him. "Daniel, you emptied out your entire piggy bank, aren't you concerned you gave too much?" Without hesitation, the young boy looked up at the pastor and announced, Nope, because I know my daddy will fill it up again." *That ain't bad theology.*

For we all must appear and be revealed as we are before the judgment seat of Christ, so that each one may receive his pay according to what he has done in the body, whether good or evil, considering what his purpose and motive have been, and what he has achieved, been busy with, and given himself and attention to accomplishing.
-1 Corinthians 5:10 AMPC

Our intentional investments advance far beyond a return in this present life. If we are now by God's great salvation going to live forever, then we have a long road ahead of us. Think loooooooong term investments. Plan ahead. Invest wisely. *Now we are talking eternal-life-hack too.*

Seventh Intentional Investment Observation
There Are Added Bonus Rewards.

Chapter Eight Conversation & Action

1. What is your favorite television commercial, and why?

2. Do you prefer to support a winning mission or a failing project?

3. How does your church effectively communicate to the congregation how their investments will accomplish community actions and great commission projects?

4. What does the life and testimony of Christ teach us about investing?

5. What prayer have you ever had answered?

6. What sentence, paragraph, or idea from this chapter do you most want to talk about?

7. Of the scripture verses listed in this chapter, which single scripture would be most beneficial to memorize?

8. In your spare time, think of someone who has invested in your life. Commit to praying fervently for them for five minutes a day for the entire week.

Chapter Nine
Milk Your Own Cow

It was hot December night in Florida. I had invested my personal night off speaking at a cake baking contest and subsequent auction. Obviously, my Dove Award status is paying off in local gigs. Typically, my client list is a little more dignified, but here, one-hundred percent of the cake money was going to a mission project.[32]   I know this mission well. The projects taken on are finished rapidly. Children in the programs from the past are now involved in the leadership. Their connections with local churches to bring about change in communities are operating wonderfully. The poor are fed daily at a garbage dump. Prisoners are visited, and orphans are ministered to. Work is being done to bring justice and transformation to trafficked children. I could go on.

A lady approached me after the event as I stood hocking my books to the impulse buying public. She began to unload, "I think we need to get all these Millionaire and Billionaire people to fix all these developing-world problems! They got all the money. They should be stepping up!" *Usually, I am very considerate and mellow, but my fuse popped.* Maybe it was because I was all hopped up on powdered sugar laced cake icing. Unfortunately, I came alive in response. "That might be one of the craziest things I ever heard." She looked shocked at my response. Maybe she is not used to people disagreeing with her. *Maybe she is single.*

---

[32] www.CupsMission.com

I continued, "I believe you might find the Bill Gates Foundation, the Warren Buffet Foundation, and the like are doing more work than many churches." She winced as I continued, "The church, my church, the people of God used to be the ones who built the great hospitals. Every hospital used to be Baptist General Hospital or Methodist Memorial Hospital, and now they belong to secular medical conglomerates. The religious name may still be on their sign, but the religion is long gone.

Her eyes got bigger and I continued, "The church used to control the great educational systems in the world, but now secular humanists have [intentionally invested] their financial resources. They now control the minds of the next generation. The church, God's people used to be the most massive charitable feeding arm around the world, now it is the secular world health organizations. The church used to be the keepers of the orphans, and that work is almost gone. If we keep letting the secular world lead in intentionally investing in social reform, we will soon have no platform to present our unique message.

By this point she was slowly backing away, so I spoke louder to make sure she heard me, "God called the church to reach the world, not Bill and Melinda Gates. But they are kicking our tails right now! We don't need the super-wealthy secular society. We need every Christian to invest in the work Christ has clearly called us to do. We have enough resources to feed, dress, and educate the entire world. Doing that would give us a great platform to present our unique message." She responded, "Well, I just think the rich need to do more and stop taxing the middle class." Then she quickly walked away. It was probably better she did. *I wanted another piece of cake anyway.* Next time someone tells me the rich need to do more I'm just going to say, "Yep."

Our joyful, intentional investments give us a fantastic opportunity to prove our gospel of Jesus is real. Our joyful, deliberate investments also give us the chance to prove to ourselves we are really part of God's reconciliation team. *Are you on that team?*

Now about whatever

Are you flat broke? Good news... intentional investments don't have to be about money. One doesn't have to have a secret vault of family money to be involved in intentional investments. We can invest our love in others. Amen? We can invest our knowledge into others. Amen? We can invest our time in others. Amen? We are [all] called and allowed to participate in intentional investments (whatever form) in other people. Our investment will become a blessing for us, and then we will turn around and invest in others more substantially.

Money is just money

Money is just linen-paper representing our time and talent and work. If I don't invest my dollars, you can safely bet I won't invest my love. Money is often a more accessible form of transferring love, faith, caring, sharing, when we cannot personally fly to South Africa. When you invest in a developing world mission, you are planting love, faith, caring, sharing, and knowledge. *Or you can take a year off work and attend language school, and then take a few years to work in the Congo.* We all have a choice. Stay with me. I am going to make a different point that you might be expecting.

If you are angry that Jesus talked about money, find a cheaper religion!

As promised, this book is not all about money, but it certainly does include money. A law is a law. It is not picky. The Law Of Increased Returns works for everything. Our narratives have been about how God takes [all] of our joyful and intentional investments and multiplies them! But what about money?

The Bible speaks very plainly about money because our hearts and our wallets are tightly bound up together, and God is after our hearts. Jesus used money and possessions as an illustration in 16 of His 38 parables. Matthew, Mark, Luke, and John, contain 288 verses... one out of ten verses deal directly with money. The Bible offers 500 verses on prayer, 500 verses on faith, but more than 2,000 verses on money and possessions.
-Howard Dayton, Crown Financial Ministries[33]

---

[33] www.crown.org

If you ever take one of my Edu-Tainment or Communication Workshops, you will learn how to tell a [live] story. You would learn how to write any story (idea/concept/parable) in five statements. Any story can be broken down to as little as five sentences. Here is our intentional investment explanation versed in two sentences...

God's unchanging Law of Intentional Investment guarantees that our joyful generous ventures into people, purposeful projects, and His church, will be returned to us with generous increased proportions in this life and the one to come. Our returned blessing will prepare us to be a blessing again.

As a believer, the most easily accessible place for you to test and prove this law to yourself is the local church offering plate. Give (invest) in your local church offering plate. Give (invest) in a great commission mission offering plate. Then share your talents and availability in the service plate to others. Maybe your church has an electronic portal rather than a golden plate, excellent. You can now feel free to type and insert with joy-filled intention. Maybe your church needs a handyman or teacher, do it with joy. Our gift (investment) is a self-test. It allows us to be convinced of the true inner faith of our own hearts.

Where your heart is, there you will also place your treasure. -Matthew 6:21

Let's recapitulate the "T" word (tithe) because most of us could swallow everything this book says, except for the "T" word being thought of as an investment. So stop trying to swallow it. Call it shareholding, or partnership, or God pockets, or grace giving. No matter what you call it, it was ordained by Mr. Grace Himself. Jesus commended the religious leaders of His day for their intentional giving while reminding them a financial gift was not the full deal.

"What sorrow awaits you Pharisees! For you are careful to tithe even the tiniest income from your herb gardens, but you ignore justice and love. Yes, you should tithe, but do not neglect the more important things. -Luke 11:42

For anyone who might think of themselves pridefully when they reminisce of their own tithing record, follow the logic. The Pharisees gave ten percent of the new leaves in their garden. Jesus agreed it was right to do. For those who claim to be genuine biblical tithe people, be sure you meet the full Jesus measurement. Move out into your back yard and trim those rose bushes. We could use some fresh flowers this Sunday. Don't be prideful and indignant! Nobody is fully [Old Testament tithing] if all they give is 10% of their paycheck.

I have fallen short in the Jesus giving category, so there is undoubtedly no judgmentalism here. We all have. But now we have been enlightened. We are called to invest greater than a financial tenth. We have been invited to bring justice and mercy for the poor. Jesus declared our investments (tithing/giving/sharing) need to include more than just money. We need a syncretized planting of everything in our life. A cash gift is starting to sound really inexpensive right about now.

As I see it, everything I have in my possession is on loan. I don't want to hold onto it too tightly. Yes, I need to be a good and faithful steward, but it is all His from the start. Everything is a re-source, originally in the hands of God. That is just the way I see it. Maybe you are not there. Okay. Perhaps I have days when my actions would not prove it either. You can call my hypocritical. *I deserve every accusation. I do hold tightly to my favorite guitars much too often.*

I don't have any sheep

Moses told his generation (Leviticus 27:30-37), the first ten percent of everything they gained, every cow and every sheep, was holy unto the Lord and needed to be invested back. If they chose not to give one of their herd, they could replace/exchange their favored furry quadruped with gold or silver representatives of equal value. *I know that was Old Testament.* The giving of their first harvested portion brought blessing upon the rest of the harvest that was to come. In this Levitical law-based society, the first portion given to God brought sanctification and protection to the rest of their crop or heard. Their demonstration that God could be trusted to complete their harvest was bound up in their giving to God first.

If the first fruits are designated holy, then the rest of the harvest is also holy. -Romans 11:16

Let us for the sake of argument, imagine the ten percent (tithe) Old Testament deal disappeared after the resurrection of Christ. *I will not fight you. I will gladly join your crusade, though you might have trouble raising the funding for it.* Today, we have the opportunity to invest even more in the bank of God and gather even higher returns. We must stop looking at shareholding in the local church as a chore and start seeing shareholding as an opportunity to harvest. We must stop looking at kindness as a chore and begin seeing kindness invested as an opportunity to harvest. We must stop looking at loving as a chore and start seeing love invested as an opportunity to harvest. We must stop looking at any investments as a chore and begin viewing investments as an opportunity plant and harvest.

Anyone can give until it hurts,
so give until it stops hurting.

We would all do well to consider ourselves as "shareholders" in our church, in our relationships, and in our purposeful missions of choice. We invest with a purpose! We attend business meetings to assure ourselves [we] have not gotten off track in what the church should be about. We carefully clarify our intentional investments have not drifted into self-serving investments solely for the comfort of the investor. In other words, we observe the church spending more on being the message of Jesus in the community than they spend on making the [well-disciple'd] comfortable? If the church is spending a majority of their resources on keeping the [well-deciple'd] happy, I will promise you those supposed [well-deciple'd] are not [well] disciples.

We make a living by what we get. We make a life by what we give. -Winston Churchill[34]

Yes, we need a new carpet, and air conditioners, and a fully equipped kitchen for our yearly Turkey day meal, as long as those actually do disciple people. At some point, the shareholders (investors) will need to observe the plan working. Shareholders are involved. Shareholders understand the organizational mission statement. For most churches, the goal is discipleship of the local community.

God reconciles the world to himself in Christ, not counting people's sins against them. God has committed to us the message of reconciliation. Tell everyone what God has done in Jesus. Help reconnect others to Him. We are officially Christ's ambassadors. God is making his presentation through us. -2 Corinthians 5:18-20

Go to the local neighborhoods and the burbs, and encourage them to come into my house, so my house may be filled. -Luke 14:23

---

[34] https://www.brainyquote.com/authors/charles-churchill-quotes

Sometimes people neglect to invest in the church for good reasons, others for silly reasons. Listen, the church has always had problems. It is overseen by flawed people like you and me, but it is still God's church. It is embraced in grace as a stumbling child learning to walk. Church problems are not new. Augustine[35] loosely lectured, "The church is a whore, but she is also my mother." The church with all of its whoring at times, its ungodly crusades, its flagrant disrespect for the example of Jesus... is still the church.

The church may be a boat full of holes, but she is the only ship that will take us through the storm. Quit talking about the leaks and bring some Flex Seal®.

Ten percent, or twenty-three percent if we go full-on Old Testament, who cares? Let's not become hung up on the percentages. Maybe ten percent is too much to trust God with. *Certainly, I am not going to give twenty-three percent.* How did that last statement make you feel?

"I would never have been able to tithe the first million dollars I ever made if I had not tithed my first salary, which was $1.50 a week."
-John D. Rockefeller[36]

---

[35] C.f. This quote has been extrapolated from his writings and used in various forms for many years. The original quote is of much greater length and definitely of identifiable comparison to the shorter version. See also https://en.wikipedia.org/wiki/Augustine_of_Hippo

[36] https://christianpf.com/john-d-rockefeller-quote-on-tithing/

I am not trying to invest the minimal amount, I am trying to invest the maximum amount of seed (love, talent, money, guitar lessons). I choose to experience the Law of Intentional Investments! Just start investing with joy.

What Happens In Vegas

I am writing a few paragraphs while seated here inside the Las Vegas International airport. *So when you think about it, what is written in Vegas must not stay in Vegas.* This airport has chosen to remain true to the city ambiance and filled the airport with slot machines. They are noisy, brightly colored, and entertaining. They are also true to their name… a one-armed bandit. Your chances of winning are slim. The odds are in favor of the house. The same goes for lotteries. Somebody has to win they declare, but they fail to broadcast how many billions had to lose to achieve one big win. I understand everyone's desire to win big. In comparison, conscientious investing is a much better bet (a pun of course) than any slot machine, poker table, or lottery ticket. *I will continue to enter the (free) HGTV dream home sweepstakes every month.* For those who enjoy buying the scratch offs… I still love you.

With the time many of us have been given, and the latest in technological tools literally at our fingertips, it is a shame that many individuals didn't accomplish more than becoming really good at Candy Crush.

You had a great meal the other day at a lovely restaurant. When the waitress brought the bill, you accepted it gratefully and reached for your wallet. Does it help to view your church offering plate as a way to say "thank you" for representing you in the community? Your church staff demonstrates your faith, your passion, and your standards to those who your own career would keep you from personally reaching. I'm just asking. I want you to taste and see that the Lord is good![37]

However, you measure your giving... give... and it shall be given back to you, compacted for more comfortable carrying, yet still overflowing compared to your initial gift. -Luke 6:38

More than a tip for thankfulness, there are still large groups of [very blessed] people like us who plant and give and invest because we need to be part of something significant! I bet you genuinely desire to meet a substantial need. I bet you want to be a superhero somewhere in life too.

I' de rather regret the things I've done, than regret the things I haven't done. - Lucille Ball[38]

I don't invest in the kingdom of God based on religious tradition. I intentionally invest in the kingdom of God based on my need to be part of something

---

[37] Psalm 34:8

[38] https://www.brainyquote.com/quotes/lucille_ball_384638

worth being a part of. I choose to experience impressive intentional returns on what I gave. I need to know I made a difference. Deliberate investments provide me with life purpose significance.

That statement haunts me, challenges me and inspires me. We are all given a portion of a lifetime. Some do great things while others only fill space. I'll bet you and I are similar. I'll bet you desire to live a life more worthy of a statue than a tombstone too. Our heart, our mind, our soul needs significance. Intentional investments of our time, talent, and resources can move us to that significant inner status. Those investments come back to us over and over again so we may find significance over and over again.

A human being would certainly not grow to be seventy or eighty years old if this longevity had no meaning for the species. The afternoon of human life must also have a significance of its own and cannot be merely a pitiful appendage to life's morning. -Carl Jung, Psychologist[39]

I think of Elio and Lorna, who went on a vacation in the Caribbean. They met a pastor who needed a house, and joyfully built one for him. Their joyful, intentional investment has blossomed into 2000+ homes built for the poor. God has increased their resources, and they have never missed a penny. I would bet these two never want for housing. Well into their eighties, there work is still going strong.

---

[39] https://www.goodreads.com/work/quotes/288698-jung

I think of Timothy, a motivational speaker who traded the spotlight to intentionally invest in a vision of significance. His joyful investment is providing clean water wells all over the developing world. I would bet this guy never finds himself thirsty.

I think of Wayne, a shoe salesman who wanted to collect shoes to help victims of Katrina. His joyful, intentional investment has turned into the world's largest shoe charity. People all over the developing world can protect their feet, and Wayne is a genuinely significant man. I have a feeling Wayne never goes to his closet and finds himself barren of shoes.

I think of John, the bookstore manager who went on an exotic fishing trip and was moved by the poverty. His intentional investment now brings medical services, dental services, biblical teaching, and hope to the Amazon River Basin. Here is a guy whose medicine cabinet is sure to be full.

I think of Nord, my Romanian friend who works hard in his home country, saving every dollar so he can spend a few months every year building churches for the poor. His life is more vibrant for having invested with the Master Builder. Meet a personally fulfilled guy.

I think of Alistair, the Guitar maker who went on a mission trip. So moved from his experience, he used Facebook to rally his friends to intentionally invest one day of their income every year to fund an orphanage in Africa. I believe his children will be well cared for.

I think of Jon and Deb, the realtors who intentionally invest in the operation of a center serving poor women and their babies in the developing world. I know God is going to take care of their grandchildren.

I think of Brianna, who at fourteen organizes a yard sale every year to build a house for a poor family. She intentionally invests her time to collect her neighbors' junk and sells it one weekend every May. She is learning business principles that will follow her forever.

I think of Franz, and his [non-Christian] German friends who intentionally invested in the construction of an orphanage. He believes his business is somehow bettered because of his investment. The law of intentional investment is universal. He knows it as fundamental reciprocity. I hope he will one day realize the good God behind the law.

I think of Tara, a single mother, while struggling to pay her own bills, sends ten dollars a month for a young girl to have sponsorship in a sewing education program. She doesn't have the extra money, but she is participating in a God-sized act that will give a young developing world girl hope and a future. This God-sized act will be a legacy for her and an example for her own daughter. She knows God will provide someone to harvest an educational gift in her own daughter.

I think of Sharon, a widow living on social security, who finds a way to send eighteen dollars a month to feed children living from a garbage dump. Talk about your widow's mite. Her container of oil has been and will be well supplied by the Supplier.

You don't have to be a superhero to act in a compassionate manner. You don't have to be a superhero to change a small part of the world.

Beyond our church offering plate and the people around our neighborhood and family, we all need to have a purpose bigger than we could imagine. We need to know we made a difference in this world. We need to bravely view all the tragedy around the world and realize we are part of a solution. We all need to know that we have personal world significance.

Our service to others brings to us great significance. Our service to others brings to them a knowledge of their God given significance.

One night, standing on a dark Dominican street, we watched a mother take pictures of her young daughter. That afternoon they had celebrated the daughters eleventh birthday, and she was now old enough to be out on the streets to raise money for the family. Sad emotions are not enough. We could have prayed for God to send someone there to rescue her. We have chosen to [be] a genuine difference in the future of many young girls in a tragic community. Having a place of [world purpose] is one of the joys of our lives. So we join with a few friends to provide third-world girls with dignity, education, and significance. Our investment gives us a heartfelt significance. If our family has any street cred (respect), it is not because I am a funny comedian, or my family is full of great musicians. Our honor is derived from our purposeful, joyful involvement in these needy children.

I desire to know that I did more than just suck air from this planet.

Great personal significance can be received when we sponsor a needy child and truly become involved in a child's life wherever the child lives. Significance can be going on a mission trip and making it become more than poverty-tourism as we allow the experience to stir us to be affirmative and ongoing action. It can be mentoring at-risk children in a low rent district on the other side of the tracks. It can be serving at a hospital, a hospice, or nursing home. It can be volunteering at the local animal shelter (God made animals). Bringing more considerable significance to others will harvest in us greater personal significance. I challenge you to live differently - invest intentionally - live significantly. At the close of most of my email I have a signature. Under my name I have these words, I want to be more worthy of a statue than a headstone.

I don't want to leave any untapped potential in my casket...

Let's fast forward to [your] closing arguments if you don't mind me referring to your upcoming eulogy flippantly. Beyond what the ministers will say about you being loved and respected, will there be an important note about your involvement in something of greatness? Will those last words declare *honestly* how your life story will live on? What will they say was your joyful, intentional successful world-changing investment? I have preached a few funerals and depending on the life of a dearly departed person, they can be tough - tough - tough! Let me preach a funeral for a genuine, joyful, intentional investor any day! That funeral is one you will talk about for years to come. One where there is a reason to mourn the loss and cause to truly celebrate their life.

That Bothersome Great Commission

We have all struggled with another interesting dilemma at one time or another. In multiple references, Jesus says, "Go into all the world and preach the gospel[40] make disciples, and baptize them..." I am sure you know the verses well. We have heard it preached for years, and we sit in our church chairs in a scripture-imposed embarrassment. Our conundrum is we realize we are not public speakers. We don't own a baptistry tank. We don't have a passport to legally leave the country and don't speak another language anyway. We only receive two weeks of vacation a year, certainly not enough time to go to the developing world and intentionally invest the time it takes to make disciples. Was Jesus asking us for more than we could produce? Was this just His sarcastic way of showing us how unworthy we are? I think not.

---

[40] C.f. Mark 16:15, Luke 14:23, Matthew 28:19-20, Acts 1:7-8

Stop! Here is another reason we love the local church. Our committed intentional investment in the local church gives us a partnership in the local portion of the great commission. Thus, we also reap the increased benefit of it. Our local church offering plate can be the first point of intentional investment in reaching the lost souls of our area. What could be the return on great commission investments? I believe if we invest in the saving of souls dear to other peoples' hearts, others will be investing in souls dear to our own hearts. That is how the sowing and reaping law works. Do you have any family that needs to hear the good message of Jesus? Invest!

I Love Waffle House

What would your opinion be if I told you I always sneak out of restaurants without paying for my food and I never ever leave a tip for a waitress? You would call me a poacher! Before you judge me... after every looted lunch, I send the price of the dinner and a generous tip to the waitress who won my heart years ago at the Waffle House in St. Louis, MO? *I would remind you she was amazing and had the menu tattooed on her forearm, and she knew my order and had it ready for me when I arrived.* The way she pronounced "Scattered, covered, smothered, and chunked," still makes me smile. Would you call me a thief, or worse? Be civil.

Don't milk another person's cow!

Invest where you are eating! I know of people who attend church in Florida and invest/support another church in Michigan, Minnesota, or Pennsylvania. *If you don't believe this is happening, ask your church finance committee!* If the church you are attending is not worthy of your financial investment, attend, and subsequently, invest in a worthy one.

Support the places that are feeding you. The last thing a senior would desire to do in the silver years of their life would be to forget to pay the bill where they are eating. You don't have to be a theologian to comprehend this. This is basic integrity. Finish strong.

Some send their full-time financial investments to a part-time or former church just so their old church knows they are a giver. Consider the negative ramifications of giving so openly. In fact, welcome to the world of the Pharisees!

Don't give like the Pharisees. Those prideful givers are nothing more than religious hypocrites seeking the praise of men. Their investment return is eaten up by their own pride. Invest secretly. Do not let others know of your great generosity. When the Father sees you giving in real secrecy, you will be rewarded. -Matthew 6:3-4

Some may believe their part-time church is not doing outstanding work. Simple fix! Become involved in leadership and help change the church to be what it should be. Be the cure. *We found out in the 1800s that a blood-sucking leech did not actually cure an ailment, and we changed the prescription.* A wise person does not spit at the

Law of Intentional Investment because they are mad at a local banker.

Decide in your own heart how much to give. Don't give reluctantly or in response to pressure. God loves a person who gives cheerfully. Then God will generously provide all you need, and you will have plenty left over to share with others. Remember what the ancient Scriptures said, "They share freely and give generously to the poor. Their good deeds will be remembered forever. -2 Corinthians 9:7-9

It is never bad to end with scripture! I really believe those last two verses say it all. It is your decision. Don't feel pressured. Legacy is a choice. This joy-filled life hack Law of Intentional Investments is here for you or you can turn it down. You decide.

Chapter Nine Conversation & Action

1. Should the uber-rich be shouldering more responsibility for the betterment of mankind?

2. Considering our own personal wealth, in light of the world's overall wealth distribution, are we hypocritical of the American wealthy?

3. Considering all the scripture that genuinely uses monetary wealth for its reference, do we

place enough emphasis on financial stewardship teachings?

4. Why should we trust God with finances?

5. What sentence, paragraph, or idea from this chapter do you most want to talk about?

6. Of the scripture verses listed in this chapter, which single scripture would be most beneficial to memorize?

7. In your spare time, consider the people/places that are feeding your faith, and contemplate any biblical reasons to re-invest in their work.

CHAPTER TEN
THREE PUMPS

I have good news! You don't have to look far to find great places to practice your joyful, intentional investment life hacking skills. The Spirit of God speaking to your heart, coupled with your joyful, intentional planting is wisdom enough. Spiritually intelligent people are going to let this law work for them by working it. Let's return to the red water pump in the middle of the dessert for one final illustration. Let's break down our [no-regret] investment life-hack points into three easy find pumps of investment.

#1 PEOPLE PUMP

Invest your time and talent into people around you. Start with one person, and then diversify into more. Find someone this week who needs your expertise and teach them how to be an expert. Find someone who really needs to be loved and love them. How will you know what to do for someone? Consider what you desire in your life right now. Plant your [need seed] in someone and watch God return it to you multiplied.

What is your gift or your talent? Will you invest your time and talent into others? Will you trust God to multiply your own abilities to you as you invest in others? Can He be trusted? Maybe it would be teaching a Sunday School class, or perhaps even taking a kid fishing. It could be showing a younger student how to play guitar or teaching a young mother how to raise children and bake cookies at the same time. Maybe it is tutoring at-risk children or starting a backyard Bible class for neighborhood little ones. I think working in the church nursery is an excellent investment.

Generous people prosper.
Refresh others and you will be refreshed.
-Proverbs 11:25

You know someone right now who could use your knowledge and insight. Call them today and ask when you can connect with them. Let them know you are fully intentioned to invest in their life. Get pushy! Investors like us invest in God's bank through our own personal investment in other people.

#2 CHURCH PUMP

Intentionally invest in your church. Your church is [your] community ministry center. Identify your trust level in God and involve yourself in reoccurring intentional financial Investments in and through the local church. You need to experience the blessings that many others already know. Christ-followers like us financially invest in God through the local church and gain the help of God returned to in similar ways. If you are already a financial partner, you might be ready to take your investment faith to a higher level. Ask yourself if God can be trusted with more?

Remember, our church partners with us in reaching the local community. If it doesn't, we don't need to withhold money, we need to help change it or attend and financially partner with a church that does.

Remember, our church partners with local foreign language groups and varied cultures in our state. These are people we would not naturally connect with. If the church is not, don't withhold money or service. Help change it or attend and financially partner with a church that does.

Remember, our church partners with developing-world missionaries to bring Christian discipleship and education to the world. If it is not, help change that, or partner with a church that does support missions.

Attending church without supporting it is the same as sending your payment and tip to another restaurant. Be a financial partner with the church you attend. Will we trust God enough to plant in His soil, the local church?

Honor the Lord with all your wealth and with an early portion of all you produce. In doing so you will be blessed in your business. Your freezer and refrigerator will be full.
-Proverbs 3:9–10

#3 PURPOSE PUMP

We all need to know that we impacted the world. It is what gives us mental permission to leave this earth with a smile when it is our time. Support or create an accountable [successful] world-changing organization. Our involvement in something special brings a greater depth of fulfillment to our lives. Maybe you are called to create something rather than partnering with another. Good! Start tonight. Tomorrow never comes; it is just today. As with any passion, it can be squashed with distractions if we don't act decisively.

You can find a developing-world mission that is genuinely doing great work both frugally and successfully. Find one that is feeding the hungry, building water wells, taking care of widows and orphans, taking care of the sick, visiting the prisoners, bringing discipleship, and baptizing people in the developing world. Get plugged in there! Educated Christian people invest in "Jesus Actions" through well-vetted, financially accountable para-church mission organizations. Stay the long haul and watch your investment make a difference.

You can find a local philanthropic organization completing great work and be a big - big part of it. Volunteer, serve on the board, clean the restrooms, paint the walls, wash the dirty children, feed the staff, or be a staff person because whatever you plant you harvest. Plant significance and harvest more considerable significance in your own life.

Refuse to let the randomness of the street corner sign-holding beggars' nickel and dime your good intentional investment funds away. Choose to find one or two good purposeful organizations to partner with. These organizations are your representatives on the foreign field. Diligently visit those third world projects and be assured the soil in which you are planting continues to produce good fruit. Know the total percentage of your gift going to actual projects. Check the integrity of the leadership.

I have received full payment, and more. I am well supplied, having received the gifts you sent. Your kindness to me is a fragrant offering, a sacrifice acceptable and pleasing to God.
-Philippians 4:18

Living an intentional life

I am a systems guy. I love to figure out how something works and duplicate it. Every well-working efficient machine you own works because it works on a duplicatable process. Your car engine, the pistons, bearings, camshaft, and crankshaft all turn in rapid revolutions, reaching thousands of RPM's (revolutions per minute). The only way your engine can do that is through a finely tuned repetitive system. The most effective way to continue a second revolution is by repeating the first revolution. Take what works and repeat it.

I know repetition is efficient. As a systems guy, I invest every month into a retirement account. I know my repeated retirement investment will benefit my future. Unfortunately, I am rather forgetful. If I did not have a pre-arranged monthly investment system, it would be September or October before I would remember to place any money aside. How do I know? Because I do not have a monthly system to pay my taxes and I always end up with a huge tax bill every April fifteenth. *Maybe I am not as smart as I would hope for people to believe.*

If systems work for engines, and computers, and retirement accounts, then intelligence will require us to attach them to our life-investments. God taught His chosen people the Law of intentional Investment early, and they remain among the affluent of the world.[41] He created tithing to demonstrate the law. He wanted his people to learn to voluntarily give a portion of their income in a systematic, repetitive way so they could repeatedly experience His automated blessing in their daily lives.

Get over it

We were reminded to be a wise systematic farmer instead of hungry hunter hoping to find a furry critter to consume. So now when you hear a church leader using the [tithe] word, don't acquire a self-imposed huff. They are merely reminding us to be that wise systematic farmer. We can joyfully invest our financial bucket in the God pump repeatedly and see the God pump work. Our leaders are reminding us about the gracious life-

---

[41] https://en.wikipedia.org/wiki/Wealth_and_religion

hack, though they may not even understand it from this perspective. If the *tithe* word bothers you, encourage your church leader to upgrade their terminology to 21rst century narratives. Explain how shareholder, investor, and partner are more biblically descriptive in today's culture... and for that matter... thousands of years ago as well.

We all need a system for our buckets. Systematic investments are pretty easy to organize. We can create an automated check for our local church or charity. We can set the alarm on our phone to remind us of the day our investment is set to transfer and offer a prayer of joyful intention to God. I certainly don't need to miss the opportunity to glorify God as I am investing with joy and expectation of His blessing.

But how about the other buckets? How can we be systematic in our people bucket and our purpose bucket? Anything that is not a habit becomes very easy to forget. Anything! When it comes to investing in people, how are we going to systematize it? I know people who use a phone alarm to remind them to stop and pray each day or share their faith. However, quality people investments often take more than a simple click task. One might [commit] to twelve weeks of nursery duty or at-risk tutoring. Investment starts with commitment. Commitment starts now.

For every successful intentional investment, a genuine effort has to be made. Priorities have been set. Goals need to be displayed in plain sight. Apathy can invade, and it is so effortless to continue through life having never followed through with our intentions. Intentions can travel in either direction. You can have great intentions unfulfilled, or you can arise every morning with a predetermined plan for greatness. Choose greatness. I know you can. I believe in you.

The intentional investments that work on a personal level also work on an organizational level. Your church, para-church group, or business needs to be investing. Why should you expect this law to be for personal use only? If I were leading a para-church ministry, I would want to find another para-church ministry to invest in. If I were overseeing a mission, I would want to find another mission I could plant into. If I were on a church board, I would want to make sure that my church was investing in a young developing church who had great needs. *Enough said.*

Magic beans?

Do you remember the children's story of Jack and the beanstalk? Those little beans could have been a gold mine. Jack should have monopolized on the opportunity with better forethought. What if the book were written differently? What if Jack was nearing forty years old and they were becoming moldy and dusty, still in his nightstand? What if in Jack's senior years he turned to adjust his sleep apnea machine and saw the bean seeds still laying in the nightstand drawer? What if the beans that had never been invested into the terra firma? Would he wonder what the possibilities could have been? Would you have wondered? *Will you wonder?*

Whoever can be trusted with very little can also be trusted with much. Whoever is dishonest with little will also be dishonest with much. If you have not been trustworthy in handling worldly wealth, why would you be trusted with genuine riches? If you have not been a good steward with someone else's property, why would God bless you with capital of your own? -Luke 16:10-12

In 2017 I accepted a special Dove Award for the little-known comedy category. Basically, it names you as the "Christian Comedian of the Year" as voted on by the Gospel Music Association and the Christian Comedy Association. After the award, a friend whispered to me, "I would give anything to win a Dove award." I responded, "I did." We are all investing everything for an outcome. We are all putting our eggs into a basket. We are all hoarding our buckets or investing them into something. We are all given a packet of magic beans. We are all being intentional about something, even if it is intentionally investing nothing. Take charge of your seeds. Along with my successes has come great failures. You are reading the words of someone who has learned the hard way. I say without hesitation that most every one of my investment failures have been on the side of not investing, rather than investing.

There is still a lot of life left in us

The invitation for each of us today is to act on our belief. We must not forget the testimony of Jesus, Paul, Elijah, and Abraham. Don't forget the testimony of secular business leaders and the testimony of everyday people who have seen the Law of Intentional Investment work in their own lives. Don't forget about corn! We have evidence! This [whatever] life-hack works!

Join me in a declaration of Intentional Investment...

I choose to invest intentionally.
I choose to invest joyfully.
I will seek for significant opportunities.
I will give - to receive - to give again.
I will share - to be shared with - to share again.
I will plant - to harvest - to plant more.
I will love - to be loved - to love more.
I will teach - to be taught - to teach more.
I will not fight the law - I will use it to my advantage.
I will not leave my magic seeds in my nightstand.
I will invest the content of my bucket into the pump.
I know my harvest comes from God.
I will give Him glory for every increase.
I am determined to hear well done faithful servant.
Amen!

I feel like a life coach after getting you to say that. Sorry. *I promise I will not start a drum circle or bring out a yoga mat.* However, we do have to encourage each other in the intentional investment direction. I hope it can be me. I hope it can be you.

Celebrate today, for your life of joyful, intentional investments, will return to you more than you can hold in this life. Those investments will overflow into the life to come. I challenge you to live a life more worthy of a statue than a tombstone. Live a life that allows them to write an authentic tribute rather than a contrived eulogy. Leave a legacy. Now progress forth and sow... whatever...

Thanks be to God who always causes us to triumph in Christ Jesus.
-2 Corinthians 2:14

Chapter Ten Conversation & Action

1. Share in your own words the Law of Intentional Investments.

2. List a few ways anyone can invest themselves into the life of another person.

3. List a few ways you or the average person can invest themselves in their church.

4. Share a few places that you personally find fulfillment in partnering with around the globe.

5. How has that partnership brought fulfillment to your life?

6. List a few ways you or the average person can invest themselves into a purposeful project around the world.

7. What sentence, paragraph, or idea from this chapter do you most want to talk about?

8. Of the scripture verses listed in this chapter, which single scripture would be most beneficial to memorize?

9. Before the sun sets today, examine how you are investing or not investing in the three critical pumps. Consider other areas that cannot be categorized by the three pumps listed.

10. In your daily/weekly/monthly devotions, re-read the Declaration of Intentional Investment to stir up the gift of God in you.

11. Leave a legacy.

About the Author

Mike G. Williams is a comedian at heart. Spend a day with Mike, and you will spend a day with a very serious guy who can bring humor into every situation. Using that unique giftedness, Mike helps church congregations experience the joy of generosity. He helps non-profit organizations raise millions of dollars for compassionate causes. He is a faithful friend and great people connector.

Mike has three desks. One is in an undisclosed location in west-central Florida. The site is far enough from the ocean to remain through rising tidal waters but close enough to be oceanfront property if global warming goes as predicted. He shares his home with his wonderful wife Terica, of 34 years consecutively. Mike makes Terica laugh, and Terica keeps Mike sane… somewhat. They have four children.

Another of Mike's desks is located at his combination office/bedroom/kitchen on the top of a small mountain in the Dominican Republic. This is home to the Crossover Cups mission, a program started by Mike and Terica started to rescue trafficked children and feed people who live at a garbage dump. Mike spends more consecutive days there than any other single place.

After five million air miles, one could say that he has a third desk. Mike writes a lot at 32,000 feet as this desk folds from the Delta® airplane seat in front of him. Many weeks a year, he is somewhere around the country speaking for the mission or taking part in a generosity stimulating event. These events help fund his work in the Dominican Republic and Haiti.

He likes to take his work on the road, so all of his documents are stored secretly on a USB key fob next to his Jeep Wrangler key. Mike has been called a comedian. Rightfully so as he garnered a Comedian of The Year award from the Gospel Music Association Dove Awards in 2017, and written material for some pretty big names in the business. He is extraordinarily improvisational and will make you laugh, any time - anywhere. Mike is a Mac® user and only uses Word® for final work sent to publishers. And he is not happy about having to do that. His formal education was in music production and has little or nothing to do with what his life's calling has delivered.

Beyond the humor, Mike is a serious soul who uses humor to keep the mind awake long enough to hear the message. Mike is an edu-tainment specialist, willing to use media, art, humor, music, drama, green chilis, and unauthorized graffiti, to teach the great truth of God's love. His staff refers to Mike as the Inspirational Educational Motivational Humorous Voice of Reason, but they believe it is a job requirement. More information is available at www.MikeWilliams.tv.